BEYOND SURVIVAL

Marriage and the Quest for Paradise

by

Ronald R. Wyse

Marilyn
Hope you enjoy these
notes for the journey
Ron

VMI PUBLISHERS

Partnering With Christian Authors, Publishing Christian and Inspirational Books

Sisters, Oregon

Published by

TrustedBooks

BOOKS YOU CAN DEPEND ON
a division of VMI Publishers
Sisters, Oregon
www.vmipublishers.com

ISBN 1-933204-01-X
ISBN 13: 978-1-933204-01-7

Library of Congress Control Number: 2005931339

Author Contact:
ronrwyse@rogers.com

TABLE OF CONTENTS

PRELUDE TO
THE JOURNEY

Some lock up their hearts, waiting for something more.

Others throw everything they've got at whoever looks good, hoping to strike gold. But a quick response sometimes springs from a shallow root. What's going to happen after the initial show of great promise?

Some insist that this ordinary-looking person is more than the dreams they've been gathering for years. The onlookers shake their heads in amazement, wondering.

Me? I climbed into the fully-loaded car, and headed off across the continent - without a map, yet.

We didn't get far before the first planned stop. After a pleasant visit and chat, we were on our way. But the second stop was in a city we'd never been to. How do we get there? Where is this place?

Finally, we stopped into a gas station and bought a map. In fact, we bought a whole book of maps. After all, the continent is pretty large.

And exactly where was our second stop located? Let's check that map. Ouch! Somewhere on the East Coast. Wow! Our final destination was the West Coast, but first thing we'd have to do is go way south and over to the east.

Good thing we got a map!

How silly, you think, to start off on a honeymoon trip across the entire continent with a full car, but no map. All packed up and heading off in all directions.

Obviously, if we were going to get to where we wanted to go, we needed a road map. Things like that get obvious pretty fast on the highway.

What about marriage? In this most intriguing and unique of all relationships, what are you hoping for? What is the destination of marriage? How will you know when you've arrived? How are you going to get there?

We all start out with some dream, however vaguely formed, or however sharply defined. Often our ideals become more sharply defined when things don't go quite like we expect them to. The excitement didn't last quite as long as we had imagined it would. She can't cook worth beans. He refuses to help around the house. Parents we swore we wouldn't "be like" suddenly come to life in our very own reactions. He's wonderful, but more dull than you could have imagined. She's not so good at second-guessing your every need like all the females did back home.

Got a road map, anyone?

Marriage is a journey. A journey of a thousand twists and turns. There are hillsides and valleys and breathtaking vistas and cliff-hanger passes. There is fair weather you could cut with a knife and spread out on a canvas, and storms which close in and leave you wondering where the rest of the world disappeared to. And in the midst of all the dilemmas and all the delights along the way, it's easy to lose sight of where we're going, and why.

The "journey" has become a popular motif in our culture. There are lots of helpful things which can be wrapped around this kind of portrayal. You can gain a sense of movement, the feeling of going somewhere—even of getting somewhere. With one brief metaphor you gain an awareness of both momentum and accomplishment. You can see beyond the daily grind to a greater end. You cease to be submerged in the innumerable details of living. The ordinary and commonplace can suddenly take on larger meanings as they're connected to a greater reason for being. At the same time, the things which constantly overwhelmed and tripped you up begin to lose their power and grip as they begin to fade away in the light of a greater purpose.

All of this is great, and can be very helpful. But movement in itself needs to be going somewhere, or else we'll fall asleep – like a baby in a steadily rocking crib. A trip to nowhere on a cruise ship might be nice for a two-week vacation, but then life returns, and it's usually pretty helpful to be able to project beyond the next two weeks of real living. Normally, when we travel, we journey from one place to another. It's natural at the beginning to know where we're hoping to end up. It's most helpful if we get clear about where we're going, and why.

This is what I tackle in the first chapter: What is the whole point of marriage? What's it all about? Unlike a trip across the country, it's not so easy simply to quickly state a single destination and move on to "how to," for people get married for a vast variety of reasons. This first, foundational chapter especially is a journey in itself, for in it we reflect on the present state of marriage, and why people stay in it, before we work towards focusing on the "center" of marriage. The "reason for being" of marriage lies beyond itself, so we begin by considering the unspeakable greatness of its ultimate destiny.

After determining the destination comes the interesting part: Getting there!

Having set the all-important stage of the "why" of marriage, having brought to light the absolute bedrock foundations of this great undertaking, what then? How can we get from here to there? Every chapter following the first one focuses on a topic which is crucial for having — or better still, for *making*—a good journey. The following overview sets the stage for what follows.

When lost, women will stop and ask for directions, men won't. True? Sometimes, especially on the road. On the other hand, I can't image a man walking into a fifteen-story building and walking up and down each and every hallway looking for Dr. Whozit's office, when he could have asked at the information desk in the front lobby. But how ready are we to check in with our Creator when we go off the main road in a relationship and get lost on some dark little side street? Do we maintain a stony silence, pretending that everything's okay, or are we willing to admit we've lost the way, that we need to realign ourselves with relational realities? Within any marriage, the need to journey from silence to confession is an ever present reality, and this is what we explore in the second chapter.

People and relationships are so complicated. Who can figure them out? Who can tell if this or that person is really a "good match"? At the edge of every scientific frontier there is mystery. There is also mystery in the center of every soul. In the third chapter we explore this unending dynamic, for there is a journey here, too. This journey entails a movement back and forth between the maze of relationships and analysis and the mystery of individual people themselves—and this is especially present in the challenge of sorting out the living together of two individuals, distinct and yet united in marriage.

And from such complexity we turn to what appears to be the simplest of scenarios – the beach. Life in the sun and the sand. Sometimes the pleasures of the five senses seem to fill the world, and we stand in danger of playing all day in shallows and missing out on things more deep and wonderful. To move from the beach to deep living may seem insane to some, to others a thrill of greater things to come. But the constant immediacy of the marriage relationship invites us forward, to deeper life and relationship and conversation.

The rugged individualist, the traditional "self-made man," seems to be always running from getting too close to others. But even a soloist is a variation on choirs and bands and group singing. "My way" may seem to me to be obviously right—in fact, perfect!—but how does that fit in with the realities of community, especially the community of two? This journey from such "perfection" to a harmonious and peaceful give-and-take of community is necessary for any true marriage to evolve.

In our sex-saturated society, it's difficult to escape the impression that having sex is no more involved than taking the dog for a walk, or doing some exercise. It's portrayed as casually as the occasional outing with a friend. Sex is pushed at us from every angle as merely being a physical sort of activity. What happened to the human soul? What happened to the depth of true friendship? The necessary journey here—not new, but always a challenge—is to move from physical intimacy to the profoundly personal.

Any athlete needs to pause occasionally just to breathe. Any sports team needs to take a "time out" to recuperate, regroup, and get ready for the next go at it. And in the midst of the swirl of activities, relationships, deadlines, obligations and all, any marriage also needs to have a breather. Most people will admit to the need of having a break, but few see how it is also so crucially necessary for a couple—as a couple—to engage, regularly, on a journey "from harassment to rest." The idea is simple, but the reality could reorder your entire relationship!

One of the constant tensions in these days is in understanding the relationship of the wife to the husband as set out in certain passages of Scripture. What are we to make of the instruction to wives that they are to submit to their husbands? And what are the husbands to do? God has gifted his Church with the Scriptures, and set us about the task of conversing seriously with one another about what they mean. In considering the journey "from slave to servant," we explore the limits and implications of this directive regarding "submission." Keeping in mind all the other journeys we're considering here, we can find something of the glory of God present in the thickness of this instruction as it is related to the depths of human relationship and motivation.

Can we discuss marriage, and the health of a marriage, without giving thought to kids? It sometimes seems like the presence, activities and demands of kids fight against the pursuit of a close marriage. In the journey "from war to remembrance," we recall the very nature of conflict, including those in the home environment. Who are the real enemies? What is it that fights against marriage? We have battles within and battles without. It is helpful to recall what's going on, especially when we're in the midst of it all!

And what about that spouse who harbors a "Messiah" complex, that amazing person who is a hero to so many? Where is there time for marriage when you're off saving the world? How do you fit "ministry" and Christian service in with a solid, dynamic and growing marriage? This is what we explore in the final chapter as we consider the journey "from Messiah to disciple."

Each chapter ends with suggestions for further reflection and "practice" related to the particular topic being discussed. These can be used by individuals, couples or groups. For reflection there are *Biblical Illustrations and Teaching*, along with comments or questions. Beyond this, there are three areas of suggestions listed under *Little Exercises*. "Little" exercises can change our lives and relationships, if we put them into regular practice.

Whether you've been considering marriage for the first time or you're presently in it—for a short while, or longer than you can remember—the time is always now to live more deeply. The goodness and wonder of marriage can be ours in ever-increasing measure, if we journey well into its fullness, in both our understanding and in our everyday living. May God himself give us light for the journey, a clear vision of our hope in him, and power to live well.

Chapter 1

MARRIAGE: IT'S NOT ABOUT YOU (!)

The Journey from Self to Center

The earth is the LORD'S.
Psalm 24:1

"Why don't we just move in together and see how it goes;
*maybe **then** we'll get married."*
"Why pretend anymore? Let's just go our separate ways."
"This marriage isn't working. I want out!"
"If you and Mommy separate, I'll go with you, and Suzy
can go with Mommy."

Marriage in the new millennium - what a mess!
Was it always like this?

It used to be that separate communities, cultures and societies had different but well-defined traditions for marriage. Marriage was a guarded treasure, with legal and social restrictions and procedures as to who would get married to whom, and when. No doubt there was some human warmth and flexibility, despite the rules of society. No doubt there was also rigidity and inhumanity. For some, the "guarded treasure" of marriage was probably more like a guarded jailhouse!

And what's happening today: paradise—or mere survival?

There are still many traditions that surround marriage, but personal survival and happiness often outweigh concern for "the others" out there. According to this view, what's really important is *self*, not *society*. Individual rights are often prized above the well-being of the larger community. And since our "community" is now the world, it's really hard to see how *my* marriage relationship can have any large-scale global effect. All over the world our lives are increasingly interrelated, but individual morality is not usually related to the bigger picture. Some movements do try to connect our everyday individual activities to larger global concerns, but these are usually limited to economic and political issues. The morality of marriage is not seen as being any greater than the two people involved.

More than this, there are wide-ranging values and movements that worsen the status and state of marriage.

Consumerism fuels our economy, and apart from the endless accumulation of goods, it poisons our whole outlook on life. In this mind-set, "What *I* want" becomes the bottom line of almost everything. We are trained in greed from our youngest days, and the habit of immediate gratification becomes normal in many areas of life, including our relationships. Advertising centers on the desires of the individual. If a market does not exist for a product or service, marketers will either create a "need," or they'll link our everyday concerns and values with the goods or services they want us to buy.

There is no God in this; no greater One to look to for trust, security, fulfillment, happiness, meaning — oh no, such things can be purchased by buying more things and enjoying more services. The West continues with its here-and-now mind-set and its materialistic solutions for spiritual problems.

It's not surprising that marriage is also perceived with "self" at the center. *My* needs, *my* wants, *my* desires, *my* fulfillment, right here and right now; all these can become the center of any relationship. These things may not be what draw us towards marriage. It's normal to enjoy enjoyment. It's great to obtain any job, or enter into any relationship, friendship, or marriage simply because we really want to. But any grasping after joy, any grabbing for happiness which focuses on "me first!" can lead to, or at least contribute to, the breakdown of relationships which is so sadly prevalent and widespread in our society.

"If I'm not getting what I want out of this marriage, I'm out!" There is no God in this view of the world—no One to whom one's deepest yearnings can be brought, for whom any desire is set aside, from whom one can obtain grace and power to live a godly life. When center stage is occupied by humanity alone, the world can quickly become empty and depressing. There is nothing greater to relate to. There is no ultimate Being who makes sense of life's joys and sorrows. The pain of personal deprivation in marriage is not counterbalanced by any sense of outside social support. Cut your losses and get out—does it make sense to do anything else?

But there are some who will try to survive a difficult marriage—"for the kids."

THE KID'S CORNER

Some will argue on behalf of the children; for their sake, stay in your marriage, put up with deprivation and neglect, stifle your potential. The shattered worlds of countless young are a strong argument for at least a truce between warring parties, between husband and wife. Some emotional security is better than none; some time together with both parents is better than no time with one of them. Between the unmet needs of the young and dependent and the natural resiliency of life, I wonder how bleak the relational landscape will be twenty years from now.

But marriage is not about children; nor are children the glue that can hold two people together. Children cannot be the bedrock of relational security, nor can they provide enough reason for trust and openness in the marriage itself. Children are not the only purpose of male and female intimacy and togetherness, nor are they the only outcome which should result from the union of body and soul. Children are too small to form the basis of a meaningful marriage.

It is the children who need to find the crucial things of life in the context of their parents' marriage: things like trust, security, fulfillment, happiness, and meaning. In the context of the family, children can learn about the larger family, the family of God. In the context of the local church, they can learn about the larger society, the society of God—which will one day fill the earth as the waters fill the sea. Much could be, and has been, said about the crucial need of children for the marriage of their parents.

It is foolish to look to the children to provide for a marriage what the marriage should be providing for the children. This completely reverses the process. Parents who rely on their children for what they should be providing *for* their children may be misguided, or possibly, irresponsible. There is no way that the young and dependent are able to give nurture and guidance, especially when these are the very things which they so desperately and fundamentally need themselves!

Just as children need to find the essential things of life by looking to their parents, so marriage needs to find the basis of these things outside of itself. The children rely on the parents; the parents need to rely on God.

The children implicitly trust their parents; their parents learn to trust God. The children find security in the faithful love and provision of their parents; their parents learn to rest secure in the unfailing love and constant provision of God. The children discover something of the fullness of life in the relational context of their parents; their parents find their fulfillment in God and in his world. The children enjoy the blessing of the secure, nurturing and stimulating home their parents create; their parents enjoy the blessing of the secure, nurturing and stimulating world that God has created. The children learn how meaningful life is, how one part relates to another, how intricately and wonderfully creation fits together; their parents learn of both the meaning and the mystery of life with God.

Of course, there's more than just the "plus" side going on.

It would be unbalanced to emphasize only the positive, created goodness of our world and relationships, and not to acknowledge the darkness as well. There is much to learn within the family relationship about the realities of sin, the need for confession and forgiveness, the necessity of growing in grace. These things and more do not cancel out the above aspects of life and learning. However, they do point to the fact that we live in a world of shadows, of incompleteness, of devastation so pervasive that we tend to see this as normal. Both the created goodness and the spiritual darkness of the greater world are part of what children need to learn in their initial world of the family. These are an inescapable part of the parents' lives, and need to be understood and reckoned with within their marriage.

Marriage is larger than children; it needs a foundation greater than just its "resultant effects," or offspring. Marriage needs a far more all-encompassing vision than just survival. It needs a context which is worthy of the grandeur of humanity; something greater than just the individual, but which in no way negates the personal in the quest for the cosmic. Before we turn to the cosmic, however, we need to consider marriage in the context of something which is both a given and a necessity — community.

One + One = Nothing

"Marriage is not about you." Marriage cannot begin and end with only one of the persons involved; it cannot even make sense with just the two involved.

In the marriage ceremony there are more than just the two individuals present; there are also family, friends, and community. There are also those who represent the Church, the people of God, and these are present not only as witnesses but are actually officiating the ceremony; they oversee the "rite of passage" into "the holy state of matrimony."

Think for a moment about a similar "rite of passage," the celebration of the entrance into life itself. I have in mind a baby dedication (or a baby baptism, which is communally very similar), when friends and family of every sort come. Dedication is not merely a moment of celebration in the midst of a weekly service — it *is* celebration, but it is not only that. The fulfillment of a baby dedication involves the ongoing involvement and presence of family, friends, community and the people of God. It is a commitment of each person present to the care, nurture, guidance and support of the young infant. Although everyone may delight in this momentary event and in the individual baby being dedicated, can there be any doubt that this entails ongoing community involvement? All share in the happiness of the new life, all rejoice, all hope for the best for its future, all play some part in its development.

So it is with marriage. In the presence of God, and many witnesses, two people vow to faithfulness. And it is in the presence of God, and in the ongoing context of many relationships — family, friends, church, society — that those vows are to be fulfilled.

It is well said that you don't marry one person, you marry the whole family. It's true. Often you also enter a new circle of friends. Moreover, people relate to you differently; you are no longer *one*. Your entire world, your central frame of reference now includes *another*. Marriage is a communal act, in that it takes place within a matrix of interrelated communities and relationships.

Marriage is also a solo act. There is an arena within marriage which—like the Holy of Holies in the temple of God—no outsider may enter. None, that is, except the two concerned. And each person enters individually. That one husband perceives and relates to that one wife in a way which is uniquely his own way. That one wife perceives and relates to that one husband in a way which is uniquely her own way. The outcome is a "twosome" which is utterly unique. This arena is the mystery of any relationship. There is a uniqueness which arises in any relationship between any two people, but there is a special uniqueness which comes into being in the marriage relationship.

As both a communal act and as a uniquely personal act, marriage is inherently relational. Relationally, marriage moves a couple into a commitment to love and to marital faithfulness. It does this by having the two getting married pledging their vows before God and before many "witnesses."

But where are we to place this intricate web of relationships?

Marriage is not about me, nor is it about you; we are not the center of the universe. The world does not exist for us, nor does it exist for our desires. We live in the setting of the world, but we are not its center. As the earth revolves around the sun, so we are to center our lives around God. Of course, we don't see all things submitted to God yet, but the ultimate destiny of all of creation is that all things will bow to the Creator. All of life needs to be seen and understood in this context.

Marriage is about God. In the context of many friends, in the complexities of family relationships, in the interrelatedness of many communities, the marriage ceremony is enacted at a local church, with representatives presiding; because in the final analysis, marriage, like all of creation, has only one true center—God.

AN ACT OF WORSHIP?

In moving from the initial starting point (*Marriage: It's Not about You*) to the conclusion (*it's about God*), there emerges an even stranger—but sharper—focus: Marriage is an act of worship.

Time out. Let's reconsider our bearings. First, we said the universe does not revolve around the earth (i.e., "it's not about you"). Next, we set forth an entirely new cosmology—the earth revolves around the sun (i.e., "it's about God"). This is powerfully radical stuff. Even for those born into the Church, the implications of this reorientation are profound. It takes a very long time to really "get it." For most, this journey extends all the way to the very last moment of their natural life!

What does it mean to say "marriage is an act of worship"? Where is this perspective found in Scripture?

Consider how the Scriptures portray the relationship of husband and wife, and how they are to regard and relate to each other. First—the husbands (found in Ephesians 5:25): "Husbands, love your wives, just as Christ also loved the church and gave himself up for her." The point of comparison here is of the husband with Christ. Christ offered up his life on the cross on behalf of the Church. Notice that it was *for* the Church that he offered himself, not *to* the Church. The offering of Christ was to *God*. As Hebrews 9:14 puts it, "Christ ... offered Himself without blemish to God."

In a similar way, Christians are exhorted to offer their entire lives up to God: "Present your bodies as a living sacrifice, holy and acceptable to God, which is your spiritual [reasonable] worship" (Romans 12:1, NRSV). The offering of all love and devotion, the offering of any service and ministry, is above all an offering to *God*.

At the very center of a husband's love for his wife, he is serving God.

The commitment of the husband to love his wife is also a specific application of the general command to *love your neighbor as yourself*. This command was called by Jesus the second greatest command (the first one being to love God; see Matthew 22:35-40). The apostle Paul used this second greatest command to sum up *all* of our responsibilities to one another: "Love . . . is the fulfillment of the law" (Romans 13:10).

This is how Ephesians continues to outline the husband's task:

> So husbands ought also to love their own wives as their own bodies. He who loves his own wife loves himself; for no one ever hated his own flesh, but nourishes and cherishes it, just as Christ also does the church ... Let each individual among you also love his own wife even as himself (5:28–29, 33).

The parallel between the general and the specific here is clear: We are to love our neighbor as ourselves, and in particular, each husband is to love his wife as he does himself.

We naturally care for ourselves. When I'm itchy, I scratch. I don't usually have to think too much about this — no seminars, no weekend enrichment weekends, no special publications, no special in-depth Bible studies are needed. I itch, I scratch. Simple.

Simple, perhaps, but in the darkness of our fallen world, in the blindness with which many of us stumble along, with all of life's many distractions, we need all the special help and reminders we can get. This is how things are supposed to be; the directive is clear, the point of similarity to how I take care of myself is easy to understand. But as Paul argued so ably (see Romans 3:23), we all fall short of the glory of God—very, very short.

Christ is our example as to how thorough-going this love is to be — to the point of the giving up of one's life. This sounds like a tall order, and it is! I can just hear many would-be husbands saying, "If this is how I'm supposed to love my wife, forget it — I'll stay single!" Perhaps you will stay single, but will you be human? Will you be "Christian"?

These directives given to husbands are just a specific application of the opening exhortation given to all Christians earlier in this passage: "Walk in love, just as Christ also loved you, and gave Himself up for us, an offering and a sacrifice to God as a fragrant aroma" (Ephesians 5:2). The directive towards husbands is, again, a specific instance of how we are *all* to love our neighbor as ourselves.

These demands could be overwhelming if we hear them from a self-centered approach to marriage. However, just as marriage is not "about you," neither are you (to put it badly) at the center of this command to love your wife as yourself. We are not at the center of the command to love our neighbor as ourselves. The center of all things is God. Before the second greatest command comes the first. This is crucial, and deserves a story to make the point.

Interlude: Martha's Love - Mary's Devotion

The story of Mary and Martha illustrates the priority of the first and greatest commandment. This can help us get a handle, and a very necessary perspective, on the second commandment to love our neighbor as ourselves. Every husband needs to have this first commandment as a clear priority if he is going to love his wife well.

Just before Luke tells us this story in his Gospel, he spoke of a lawyer asking Jesus how he might "inherit eternal life" (see Luke 10:25-42). Jesus asked him how he understood the law, and the lawyer basically responded with these two commands: love God, and love your neighbor. Jesus commended this answer, but when the lawyer tried to get overly particular about "who is my neighbor?", Jesus gave the well-known parable of the Good Samaritan. Following his recounting of this entire incident, Luke inserted a small snapshot from the lives of Mary and Martha. The resulting arrangement looks something like this (Luke 10):

> *The lawyer mentions the 1st command: love God*   *v. 27*
> *He notes the 2nd command: love your neighbor*   *v. 27*
> *Jesus illustrates the 2nd command with the*
>   *Good Samaritan parable*   *vv.30-37*
> *Luke illustrates the 1st command with the*
>   *Mary and Martha story*   *vv. 38-42*

Mary and Martha were sisters, and good friends of Jesus. In this story, Martha welcomed Jesus and his disciples into her home, but as she busied herself preparing for her "honored guests," she became distracted, worried and bothered. In fact, she spoke rather impudently to Jesus, even as she referred to him as her "Lord" (v. 40). She questioned Jesus' concern for fairness and demanded that he order Mary to help her! In his gentle reply, Jesus spoke words which have become famous in the struggle between a life filled with "spiritual" devotion and the necessity of "ordinary" work: "Only a few things are necessary, really only one, for Mary has chosen the good part" (v. 42).

Although much has been written about how these sisters may represent "spiritual" devotion vs. everyday work, my concern here is to highlight Luke's unique use and placement of this story—for this short tale occurs only in Luke's Gospel. Luke uses Mary's devotion to Jesus to illustrate the first commandment, just as Jesus told the parable of the Good Samaritan to illustrate the second commandment. Martha did not "fail" because she was concerned about properly serving her "neighbor" (in this case, her guests); such service was natural, expected and completely appropriate. Her problem was that, for whatever reasons and however momentarily, she was more preoccupied with the "love of neighbor" than with the "love of God." Mary, on the other hand, had her priorities straight.

First things first. At the center of our "love of neighbor" must be the "love of God."

To whatever extent we are focused more on our service *for* God than our relationship *with* God, to that extent we are in danger of becoming distracted, bothered and worried—just as Martha did. The first priority is always God. Loving people is crucial: "The one who does not love his brother whom he has seen, cannot love God whom he has not seen" (1 John 4:20). But in terms of what is central, loving others can—or should—only occupy second place. This ordering of value and concern can help to place the demands of Ephesians into context.

What Happens to Me?

My love for my wife must be seen as a part of my larger devotion to God. If this priority is not in place, then we may well get overwhelmed with the incredible demand of loving another person as naturally as we look out for our own interests. To make matters worse, the "person" in question is not some distant neighbor, but someone inescapably near at hand. With the example of Christ, I love my wife as an act of devotion. And this is not, first and foremost, a devotion to my wife — it is an act of devotion to God.

Neither myself, nor my wife, are at the center of the command for me to love my wife "as Christ loved the Church" and "as I [naturally] love myself." This love and devotion to another person is an act of devotion, an act of service, an offering rendered unto God. This activity of love is not centered on *my* needs, *my* wants, *my* desires, *my* fulfillment; nor is it centered on *her* needs, *her* wants, *her* desires or *her* fulfillment. The center of this activity is, rather, devotion to God. The "love of God" is always to be the goal for "the love of [and service to] neighbor"; from the nearest neighbor (my wife) to the most distant (the needy on the other side of the globe).

It is in this sense that marriage can be understood as an act of worship. As Christ loved the Church and sacrificed himself to God for the good of the Church, so I am to love my wife by sacrificing myself to God for my wife. I am to look out for her interests as well as those of myself, and in this way follow the example of Christ who emptied himself of all his natural rights (see Philippians 2:3–7).

Someone may well object, "But there will be no *me* left!"

Good point, and well said. Actually, I might better put it this way: Good point, well and *truly* said! In a way, we're repeating what we've already covered.

What do I mean? That *being Christian* needs to precede *being married* (precede in priority, of course, not necessarily in chronology). If we have already given ourselves to God, if we have already embarked upon that unending journey in response to the call of Jesus—that call which says disciples must "deny themselves and take up their cross and follow me" (Mark 8:34, NRSV)—then the requirement of loving my wife is just a case in point. Because of the immediacy and constant nature of the marriage relationship, this is sometimes a very challenging case in point, but in the end it is only a specific application of the general instruction for every Christian in every place with respect to every other person: love.

As part of my worship of, and service to, God, I have vowed and dedicated myself to loving my wife. Beyond the delight I naturally found in knowing her, beyond the reasonableness and evident good sense of our union together, I took the definitive step: I vowed before God (and others) to love her always.

This dedication to love her does not diminish the natural wonderfulness of knowing her; rather, it both insures that the initial and formative "wonder" remains and causes our relationship to expand and deepen "worlds without end." To paraphrase the old hymn writer, "Have you not seen, how your desires ever have been, granted in what He's ordained?" (Neander). The world is afraid that doing what God has set out for us will bring about a cursed, darkened existence. But actually, to rework one of Hudson Taylor's sayings, "God's will, done in God's way, does not invoke a curse, but rather, a blessing."

That husband who denies his natural self-interest, and expands his concerns to act in love towards his wife — all the while keeping God as his top priority — that man will experience the blessing of community, of being in relationship; in a word, of *marriage*.

SAME COIN...DIFFERENT SIDE

In the same passage of Ephesians, the wife is addressed with much the same orientation: "Wives, be subject to your own husbands, as to the Lord....As the church is subject to Christ, so also the wives . . . to their husbands in everything....Let the wife . . . respect her husband" (Ephesians 5:22, 24, 33).

These words were certainly not penned in the twenty-first century! I find that merely mentioning them here, done with the desire to treat this passage as an integral whole, threatens to open a Pandora's box of modern concerns. And even beyond the realities of the changing roles and perceptions of men and women in society, there are all also the current varieties of church government and functioning all based — so they claim — upon the New Testament, which raises questions about how the church is, or should be, submitted to Christ.

The issues are complex and much-discussed, but it is not my intention here to focus on these concerns; rather, my concern is to refocus marriage on God. What has been said above pertains to wives as much as it does to husbands. At the center of marriage cannot be the needs, wants, desires or fulfillment of the individual; this applies fully to the wife as well as to the husband.

According to this passage of Scripture, as the wife has already submitted to Christ—which includes her needs, wants, and desires—so she is to enter and continue in the marriage relationship. Of course, submission to Christ is a life-long journey, a commitment and a progress. But once again, the reality of marriage brings the issue of the first commandment into sharp relief: How have we progressed in loving God above all other loves?

The fears of being "swallowed up" by a husband who places his own desires at the center of the relationship are real and well-founded. Whereas "Hell" is, in part, being consumed by your own desire (speaking experientially), being consumed by another's desire more quickly *feels* like hell—as many in the midst of it all would put it. In the end, the agony is similar, as it centers upon desire. But in the case of being profoundly unfulfilled, there is the agony of deprivation, an experience which we usually feel more deeply than the long-term benefits of fulfillment. (I suspect that—after the initial rush of ecstasy—most of us quickly adapt to positive situations, and then get on with life.)

With the emphasis on women's issues and rights in recent decades, the world may have succeeded somewhat in removing the husband's desire as the controlling factor in a marriage. But what progress have we made if marriage is now dominated by the wife's desire? If all of our hopes and dreams, plans and ambitions, are to be surrendered fully to God upon the altar, removing self-serving power from one party, only to give it to another, brings forth no Christian gain. In the name of justice, one form of darkness would have then been exchanged for another.

If the world sees submission to God as death, how could it ever see a wife's submission to her husband—done because of her more fundamental and primary submission to Christ—any more favorably? However we are to translate this exhortation for the wife into practical terms, the spirit of it remains: For the wife, marriage is an act of worship grounded in her prior submission to God.

As I write this, I feel the anger of injustice, of subordination, of negation; such experiences are not the sole domain of any one group of people. They are all too common—throughout the world, and down the street! For women, how can one accept the general principle of this exhortation without first dealing with its practical implications? There are considerable issues surrounding the interpretation of this text, far too many for me to deal with in this chapter. In order to keep the present focus clear, I have limited myself to making and exploring the one central point: Marriage is an act of worship. The important and related details of "What does it mean to submit?" will be explored later (in chapter 8).

Submission to the calling and work of God often comes long before any understanding of what it all means. Likewise, in marriage, if we knew all that lay in store, many of us would quit even before we began. Indeed, the negativity and fallout from many marriages discourage countless people from even embarking on the journey. No one can understand *all* that a particular path, a specific vocation, that one relationship, will entail before embarking. We usually have enough of an idea to entice us onward; exhaustive details about potential "challenges" only kill the vision.

In accepting this point about submission, one doesn't need to accept that marriage in general—or marriage to a particular person—is necessarily "God's will." The question of how a specific relationship may affect a woman's own growth and development is separate from this understanding of marriage as part of her devotion and service to God. If there is fear of becoming a "non-person," then perhaps the man in question hasn't persuaded her that he will love her as Christ did the Church.

The calling of God for the wife in marriage is to submit herself to the love of Christ as it is conveyed through her husband. Although each husband is imperfect, incomplete and sometimes even malformed, so also is each church, pastor and spiritual leader. This is simply the way we are; we need always to mature and grow in Christ.

Nevertheless, there is an order to this process. Both husband and wife are, first of all, committed to God in all things. Then, and only then, can they be committed to each other "for better or for worse." In this way it is God himself, and not the imperfect "other," who is then the center of their marriage. This is the crucial thing, the priority, the first command, firmly set in first place: getting right in our relationship with God. Following this, the second thing— getting right in our relationship with others, including our spouse—takes its proper place.

Love, Death and Marriage

In giving his life for the Church, the goal of Christ was to deliver us from darkness, futility and slavery. It is ironic that many see marriage as a complete reversal of this process. Many see the "bonds of matrimony" as a form of slavery, a futile attempt at securing happiness, a quick trip to oblivion. "Another one bites the dust!"

Like the relationship of Christ with the Church, the husband's mandate is to nurture his wife *from* all darkness, futility, and "slavery," and to lead her ever upward into the brilliance of God's light, to fulfillment, to freedom. "It was for freedom that Christ set us free; therefore … do not be subject again to a yoke of slavery" (Galatians 5:1). We must be always attentive to the necessity of moving onward from our darkness to God's light, for ourselves and—in the context of marriage—for one another.

The journey which culminates in true marriage, this journey from self to the Center, has been charted out for us in Scripture. We take the plunge and make a vow of love and commitment on our wedding day, but this is only the beginning. For a true, thorough-going, heart-to-heart and soul-to-soul marriage to come about, this requires "death." Not our own death, but death to things which compete against true marriage. As we die daily to our instinctive self-preoccupation, we are enabled to become more alive to others, and gradually we grow into the blessed depths of becoming ever more married.

As the husband dies to self, surrendering self to God on behalf of his wife, he will be enabled to love his wife—as naturally as he cares for himself and as thoroughly as Christ loved the Church. As the wife dies to self, submitting herself to Christ, the Lover of his Bride, she will be enabled to submit to her husband as God intends. All of this, on the part of both husband and wife, is an act of devotion, an act of worship, primarily rendered unto God — for whom and to whom are all things. And for both, this ongoing commitment will usher in the very blessing of God: blessed are those who hear the word of God, and do it (Luke 11:28; Marshall, 482).

Biblical Illustrations and Teaching

1. At the beginning of this chapter, I quoted from Psalm 24 ("The earth is the LORD'S"). This psalm focuses on God as central, and on the requirements of those who would come near to him. If God is also central to marriage, how can this psalm affect your view of your marriage?

2. In John 13:1–20, Jesus demonstrated to the disciples how they were to serve one another. In reading the passage, notice how Jesus' actions were based upon his relationship with God (v. 3). How does your relationship with God affect your ability to "serve" your spouse?

3. Paul told his readers to give themselves to God as living sacrifices (Romans 12:1), and he added, "Do not be conformed to this world, but be transformed by the renewing of your mind" (v. 2). What aspects of "worldly thought" referred to throughout this chapter do you recognize as being within yourself? What perceptions need to be renewed?

Little Exercises

1. To help in the process of putting God first and spouse second, try praying the Lord's Prayer (Matthew 6:9-13) "into" the life of your spouse (e.g., "May Your name be made holy in the life of _____; " 'Forgive us our debts' — and I pray that You would forgive _____ his/her debts, as he/she forgives...").

2. In the course of reading this chapter, you may have noted a number of ideas which contrast with, affirm or expand your views of marriage. Reflect on or discuss these ideas. Are they sufficiently biblical? (Usually, no one passage "says it all.") How might they affect you—in thought, word or deed—with respect to marriage?

3. Take some time to reflect on the relational context of marriage: family, friends, community and church. How do the "regular" people in your life affirm and help your marriage? How might some speak or work against it? In what ways can you embrace the helpful aspects more fully, and stand against the destructive ones more strongly?

Chapter 2

THOSE THREE LITTLE WORDS

The Journey from Silence to Confession

Be kind to one another, tender-hearted.
Ephesians 4:32

People are so irritating. At least, *other* people are, occasionally. It's amazing how annoyances can arise — some completely unscheduled, some completely predictable. The predictable ones may lead us to either a good-humored shake of the head with a knowing, "There she goes again!", or they may lead us to a cumulative buildup of resentment. The unpredictable ones, well, they happen all the time.

And how do we deal with life's irritations? Sometimes we completely miss it; the offence passes by harmlessly while we're looking the other direction. At other times, we can fly into a sudden rage over what was actually an entirely innocent and completely unintended slip.

One psychologist and writer, reflecting no doubt on years of clinical and personal experience, made an insightful comment which relates to this dynamic: "I suspect that many people hold their lives together by denial" (Crabb,

Understanding People, 67). This certainly applies to many relationships; and the closer the relationship, the more applicable it can be.

In the context of a sad moment of American history, this tendency towards denial was put in memorable form by comedian Jerry Seinfeld. On the question of whether President Bill Clinton had lied about having sex, Seinfeld joked, "People lie before, during, and after sex"—the obvious implication being, "So, what else is new?"

Lies and denial, cloak-and-dagger, shifting shadows; I am not what I appear to be. Most assuredly, we live in a world which prefers darkness to light, secrecy to openness, duplicity to plain dealing. We use speech to gain our own ends; we maneuver and plot like we're in a cosmic chess game. We recall and rehash past conversations, second-guessing what the other, or others, were *really* saying.

And how does all of this play itself out in marriage?

This cuts to the very heart of a marriage relationship. Marriage is about two people gradually moving closer and closer to one another. As the days, months and years go by, layers upon layers of intimacy are slowly unwrapped. No two people can know each other like an old couple who've been "through it all" together. When the young diamond in the rough has finally been smoothed to a beautiful luster, the beauty of a refined character can finally sparkle.

This glowing result may sound great, but how does it happen? Does character become refined through lies and denial? Can intimacy deepen when the inevitable cuts and bruises of an everyday relationship are overlooked and ignored in silence? Of course not!

The way towards the "promised land," towards the hoped-for paradise of relational intimacy and joy, can only be reached on our knees. To reach the heights, you must travel the depths. The way forward in any relationship cannot be done in silence, but in the light of confession. "Confess your sins to one another, and pray for one another, so that you may be healed" (James 5:16). "Confess" is simply a fancy term for admitting something we'd rather pass over in silence. Sounds tough, and it is! But it's not impossible, and it sure beats hiding in the shadows, rather than out in the clear light of an intimate, honest relationship.

MUCH SHADOW, LITTLE COMFORT

Both within and outside of marriage, the light of day can be a painful experience. Sometimes our kindest intentions are simply not seen, for lack of observable results. At other times, our subjective version of a conversation may hit reality when the *actual* words said, the *actual* deeds done, are pointedly recounted by the other(s) involved. Eventually, for each one, wrinkles appear, revealing inescapable aging; bad news for those who idolize youth and beauty! It is hard to welcome truth.

The light which shines *around* us, illuminating our world and the worlds we live in, is endlessly welcome—as the endless media attests. It's wonderful learning about all kinds of things. Our world is so utterly fascinating, people are forever discovering new aspects of our lives, the planet, our universe. Moreover, we are always so deeply interested in ourselves: personality theories, leadership and learning styles, who is doing what with whom, what are the most recent developments in every kind of endeavor imaginable.

It is the light which shines *upon* us which we prefer—ever so desperately—to avoid. We freely criticize others, and just as freely forgive ourselves. We suspect the worst of motives for the most innocent behavior, yet are astonished at how others cannot see our good intentions in even our most serious blunders or oversights. We justify our own guilt, and condemn the innocent from a distance.

We prefer shadows to light. Even when we come close to clearing up a strained friendship, we back off. A half-hearted, awkward and incomplete apology (like, "Um, about, ah, what I said back there. . .") is met with a hastily uttered, "It's okay!" This is followed by an almost annoyed and embarrassed, "Don't worry about it." Worse, the incident may be counter-balanced with a gift, of sorts. We know the offender feels bad, so we give or do something which the other likes, to show we're not really offended, as if to say, "It's okay—let's just not *talk* about it!"

Even fairly good relationships sweep too much dust under the carpet. None of this "speak the truth in love" stuff (an ancient exhortation, located in Ephesians 4:15); just accept that people are different, look on the bright side, count your blessings, swallow your pain.

It is hard to live as Christians; we are born in darkness, we are nurtured in darkness, and in turn we embrace darkness. We call it a coping strategy. We explain it historically by looking to the distant causes of war, depression or misguided idealism, anything but the culmination of spiritual darkness, of shadows here and shadows there, gathering through generations of family and social history. Darkness is so normal we think that we live in the light; our society isn't that bad, our family is normal, our church represents the most important part of the truth and good Christian practice.

And so we live second-rate lives and hope to survive second-rate marriages, never guessing that on the other side of the unthinkable lies an undreamed of freedom. In the shifting shadows of our lives, we both advance and retreat. We stand tall because we cannot conceive of bowing low. We polish our shields and armor, for to give away our weapons would be certain death. Even when we are physically close, we distance ourselves within ourselves; retreat into darkness, shun the light, and everything will be all right—or at least, livable. Absence of conflict is preferable to dropping our guard, to admitting wrong, to acknowledging pain.

But the shadows are a poor substitute for real living and a real relationship. Better the warmth of true light than the isolation of a shadowy existence. But how do we get from here to there?

Just Say It

"Please forgive me." These words are far from our lips. They do not come easily. Several things precede them, several things may follow them. They change the very nature of relationship. They war against darkness. They war against pride. They savor of grace.

Surely Christ died needlessly—we did not, and we do not, need such a pure sacrifice. We have done no wrong. Is this what we think? Is this how we behave? "This is the way of an adulteress: she eats, and wipes her mouth, and says, 'I have done no wrong'" (Proverbs 30:20, NRSV). We are that adulteress. "Who can say, 'I have cleansed my heart, I am pure from my sin?'" (Proverbs 20:9). We can, and we do.

We are full of reasons and excuses. This is our starting premise. We say, "I was not wrong." Moreover, we say, "I am not wrong" (echoes of 1 John 1:8, 10 — "We have no sin....We have not sinned"). There are excellent reasons why we spoke, and behaved, so badly. "If you only knew the pressure I'm under, the people I have to deal with, the impossible expectations imposed upon me, the deficiencies I grew up with.. . ." And on the list goes.

Of course, there are other ways of avoiding the truth. A popular one is by admitting to a lesser crime. It wasn't an outburst of anger, one of the "deeds of the flesh" (Galatians 5:19-21). Oh no — I was just "grumpy." And aren't grumpy (old) men so adorable, just like a grumpy little baby? This is our own whitewashed interpretation of what happened. "I am innocent of this Man's blood" (as Pilate said of Jesus, Matthew 27:24); and from there we build our innocence of all bloodshed.

Face the light. Turn truth-ward. Bend the knee. Acknowledge wrong. Ask for forgiveness. Break new ground. Refuse darkness. Humble pride. Taste freedom. Savor joy.

A CONVERSATION IN PROGRESS

How many times have I (represented by the "R") had the following conversation with my wife (shown by the "S")? More times than I wish to recall! Each time it's as hard as the last time. It goes something like this:

R. "I'm sorry. I shouldn't have done that. I shouldn't have said that. I was wrong. I am sorry. Please, forgive me.

"No, don't brush it off. Don't pretend nothing happened. We're distant. You've retreated. We're not close. Please, forgive me.

"It's okay, you don't have to do it right now. Take your time...you've got until sundown."

Response #1 — many times, after a great amount of discussion

S. "I forgive you."

R. "Really??"

S. "Of course. I have to, or else I won't be forgiven."

R. "Are you sure?"

S. "Yes."

R. (After a pause) "Seal it with a hug 'n a kiss?"

S. "Okay."

Response #2 — at other times

S. "I'm trying, but it's hard. I'm really shocked. How could you say that? You're a Christian! I'll be okay — just give me some time."

Perhaps I should explain a few things about this dialogue. Our conversations in seeking and offering forgiveness — really, even *talking* about it — have been affected by two Scripture passages. The first is found in Matthew 6:14–15 (which follows hard on the heels of the Lord's model Prayer), where Jesus says: "For if you forgive others their trespasses, your heavenly Father will also forgive you; but if you do not forgive others, neither will your Father forgive your trespasses" (NRSV).

I once heard a well-respected Bible expositor preach on this passage. Because these verses can sound like "works-righteousness," this speaker so distorted the plain reading of the text he ended up saying, "We can forgive, since God has forgiven us." I'm not actually sure how this passage ties into God freely forgiving us (explanations vary), but I cannot escape the necessity this text clearly lays out for us to forgive.

In the day-to-day ebb and flow of our own marriage, we have come to regard forgiveness as a God-given necessity. Perhaps I should say it is a God-*imposed* necessity; it certainly does not come naturally, or easily, nor is it a welcome discipline. As Christians, we are bound to forgive one another, and that applies within the marriage relationship as well as outside of it.

Scrapes, Bruises, Wounds

Forgiveness is not cheap, nor is it easy.

Unintended hurts are easier to forgive, sometimes, depending on the depth of the pain brought on. If I dropped a desk chair on your foot, it would probably hurt! No doubt I would stutter a thousand apologies, sit you down, and ensure that you're going to be all right. And how would you respond? Your foot would likely feel fine after a short time. If the pain is not deep, if it is short-lived, if the pain was unintentionally given, then forgiveness will likely come easier.

If, however, I intentionally hurt you—raising my voice, or quietly cutting you down—forgiveness may be more difficult. If the pain becomes suffering, and the suffering endures, what then? It's not only small children who can die from neglect; any one of us can wither from relational deficiency. Deep suffering brought on through cruelty or through carelessness, done deliberately or done in ignorance — this is harder to forgive.

Some actions, and some words, are slight; others rip and tear. Things spoken or done in haste, in the heat of anger or out of personal pain, can leave another person devastated. It is not lightly that anyone can speak of "the necessity of forgiveness."

In the above conversation between "S" and "R," the hurt experienced was real hurt; not disastrous, but nevertheless real. The need for requesting forgiveness *was* necessary; otherwise, the relationship would have soured. It wouldn't have soured completely, or all at once. But if "one bad apple can spoil the whole barrel," what will ten do, or twenty? The effect of even one blow to a relationship will be to weaken it; and that weakness—small as it is—will remain. Yes, it will remain until it is dealt with.

Of your own offence, you may say, "It was such a small thing. It was nothing. Why go through the discomfort of bringing it up, of even mentioning it?" But is this yours to decide? If—or perhaps I should say *when*—we have offended our spouse, we must do the difficult thing. We must step out of the shadows into the light. We must put our offence on the table in plain view. We must open the conversation. We must humble ourselves. Let the other decide if our offence is trivial.

But, beware: It is hard to ask for forgiveness. It is hard also to give it. It is hard to admit to personal pain on either side. It is difficult to reveal vulnerability. And in a day when superficiality is commonplace, it is hard to say, "This matters; this is important. I have been hurt. I've been wounded. I cannot carry on as if nothing has happened."

Forgiveness can take time. It can take time to move from denial of hurt even to some awareness of it. It can also take time to move from an initial growing awareness to a full acceptance of emotional and relational pain. In the second alternative ending to our conversation (response #2), "S" says, "I'm trying (to forgive you), but I'm in shock...give me time." The request for time is evidence of the depth of a marriage relationship, and therefore of the hurt a rupture to that relationship brings.

A boxing match often ends with one of the contestants—weary, hot and sweaty—finally landing a knockout blow to the other's jaw, and down he goes. Only after the count of ten is a victor announced. We expect the loser of the match to slowly come around, take a few moments to refocus, gradually realize what happened, and then, slowly and painfully, get up and drag himself off.

Not so in relationships! A heated argument may drag on through several phases, and finally the fatal blow is landed. Somebody wins, and somebody loses. What then? Then we expect—insanely enough!—that things should quickly go back to normal. "Business as usual." We shut our eyes to the blood, the sweat, the tears. The relationship takes (another?) turn for the worse. What distance, what a chasm, lies between our proud stance over our vanquished foe and the act of contrition, of humiliation, of obedience, of saying, "Please, forgive me...."

Or, worse still, we may ice over the suffering and go straight for a "please forgive me" type of line, without actually admitting wrong, without feeling the suffering we have brought about. In acting or speaking as if "nothing has happened," we can pretend to be reconciled. It doesn't work, though. It cannot work. The labor of love necessitates the pain of admitting wrong, the pain of admitting suffering, and the humility of requesting that the other forgive you.

It's Always Now-O'Clock

Before we lose sight of the dialogue, I need to mention one other point embedded in our conversation which relates to the timing of forgiveness. Sometimes Sarah and I—somewhat jokingly—say, "You've got until sundown." We especially may say this if the other is hesitating, perhaps because an old wound has been re-opened. Old pains have a way of being suddenly present, and the process of confessing and forgiving needs to slow down enough to allow time for the realization and admission that an offence or blunder has gone deeper than one would naturally expect.

This expression about sundown is a spin-off from Ephesians 4:26, where the instruction is given, "Be angry, and yet do not sin; do not let the sun go down on your anger." This verse is not directly related to forgiveness. However, to the extent that we are exhorted to deal with anger on the same day it arises, so likewise it is expedient to deal with the things which so easily give rise to anger. And what can evoke anger as easily as an injustice suffered? Not forgiving an injustice opens the door, or perhaps ensures that the door stays open, to anger.

It takes a lifetime to become Christian. For some, it may have only taken a moment to become a Christian, to see the light, to start the journey. But for everyone who has called upon the name of the Lord, there is a never ending process of growth. Dealing with anger and its causes in the present moment does not suddenly wipe the slate clean. We unconsciously—but invariably—expect what is our due; and in marriage we sometimes magically expect the other to keep the covenant of committed love without faltering in any way. Learning to love, and learning how to be in an intimate relationship, does not happen overnight. It takes a lifetime to become married. The moment of commitment clears the way for a lifetime of learning.

Part of the learning is living in the present tense of relationship. It entails the deliberate determination to deal with things as they arise. As in a waltz, to move responsively together you need to continuously keep in touch. But if he's constantly stepping on your foot, hard, it's pretty hard not to back off somewhat. In relationships, the deeper the hurt, the harder it is to keep close. "Once burnt, twice shy," my father would often say. The goal of keeping in touch sometimes necessitates some breathing space, but eventually the aim is to reconnect.

The movement towards reconnecting, towards reconciliation, is not always natural. In fact, it is thematic of this entire chapter that this goal is unnatural, it is uncommon, it is not a normal practice. Reconciliation is radically Christian. It is countercultural. It is revolutionary. It necessitates truthfulness and commitment. It is an integral part of becoming Christian; it is an integral part of becoming truly married. The time is always *now* to deal with anything which has separated you from your spouse.

RADICAL CHANGE

The request for forgiveness moves any relationship from the basis of pride to the basis of grace. There is nothing I can do to undo harm. I am incapable of removing pain, and no one can move into the past to remove the shocking pain of a past injustice suffered. In the request for forgiveness, I am requesting that the relationship be reestablished by the other; the one whom I have hurt, the one whom I have damaged, the one whom I have neglected.

I cannot, by my own activities, reopen the lines of personal connectedness. The other person may be suffering, in shock, deprived, needy, weakened, numbed, bewildered, disillusioned, beset by sin and temptation, imperfect in understanding, incomplete in faith, deficient in hope. Nevertheless, I request unmerited favor. I dare to hope that the other person will graciously rise out of the ashes of the shame of their pain and humiliation, extend the "right hand of fellowship," and release me from my debt by refusing to grasp after their rightful claim of unconditional love, justice and respect.

Is it any wonder that little is truly forgiven in marriage? We are expected to be Christian, but in truth we are a bad mixture of light and darkness in every respect of our every relationship.

Some churches seem to stress only the beginning of faith, and not the process. Are you saved, or not; are you in, or out; have you accepted Christ, or rejected him? These are fine questions, if balanced with teaching on the rest of Christian growth. A similar thrust can be found in the wisdom of Proverbs, where the central choice of life is worded in a tale of two ways: wisdom, or folly. Likewise, the gospel can ask, "Do you accept Christ, or reject him?" There are moments of decision which can cast a shadow, or a light, over all the remaining years of one's life.

But once you're in, once you've shifted your center from Self to God, once you've re-aligned your fundamental allegiance, then what? I grew up in a church tradition which—in my experience, at any rate—answered this question very poorly. There was so little teaching, or training, in the process of godliness. Back then, the spiritual disciplines which can aid in one's progress in faith, hope, and love were not anywhere on the horizon; at least, the horizon to which I was exposed. "The Faith" seemed more cognitive, more between-the-ears, than it did life-related and life-changing.

Surely the Christian faith is all-encompassing: We rejoice over a new birth, and we rejoice over growing maturity. Outer growth includes efforts to spread the gospel in both evangelistic word and in loving deed. It needs to do this. But it cannot only focus on works out there, while neglecting development back home. The Christian home cannot merely be a building containing biologically-related people who all agree to a generally-accepted view of the world. For a home to be Christian, each person in it must necessarily be "expanding the area of his conversion" (Foster and Smith, 303). Each relationship must be an arena wherein we seek to become every increasingly Christian.

It was the blood of the Holy One of God that made our relationship with God possible. Blood cost life. In each moment, we need that forgiveness. The posture implicit in the Lord's Prayer is a necessity for all relationships; it is no less crucial for marriage. "Forgive us our sins, for we ourselves forgive everyone indebted to us" (Luke 11:4, NRSV). No ongoing, close relationship can continue or become deeper without the constant practice of forgiveness.

Deeds Also Speak

Repentance without change is meaningless. To say, "Please forgive me," without admission of real guilt, real liability, and real offence is equally meaningless. For those whose words slide off their lips with effortless ease, who are past masters of verbal duplicity, whose conversation flows like shifting shadows, the challenge may well be to stand long in the clearing of confession.

To be where you are means to take a stand in these words, to leave the shadows and come to the light, to accept the sentence that wrong has been done and that *you* did it. Repentance is a moment; it is also a way of life. It clears the way for new direction. In marriage, it can bring in more light and clear away more fog. It can restore the joy, and enjoyment, of the other person and of your life together.

However, repentance with change does not make sense if it is only "in general." We sin in particular—in particular thought, specific word, and tangible deed—and we need to repent and change at the same level of specificity. Repentance as a way of life means we are determined to change. Repentance as a moment means that right here, right now, I confess to a particular misdeed. I apologize. I ask your forgiveness. And I will—if I'm smart enough to think of it— ask for you to pray for me in this specific regard.

No relationship gets as detailed on a daily basis as marriage. There is always the need to give, to flex, to grow, to allow. In the midst of it all, it is always too easy to neglect the other, to place your own concerns, your own way of doing things, above the other. There is so much opportunity to practice this spiritual discipline of forgiveness, this necessity of the Christian life.

The practice of requesting, and granting, forgiveness should be as much of our daily routine as brushing our teeth and taking out the garbage. It keeps the relationship clean, because it so easily gets cluttered up. It keeps it clear, so the natural conversation about things trivial and things profound can continue onward and upward. It keeps it tender, so the happiness, the spark, the implicit blessing of this relationship can grow and deepen.

GRANTING FORGIVENESS

The immediacy of pain, the ongoing shock of suffering, can make forgiveness a challenging task. Moreover, if time has passed and the offences have become so numerous and varied they escape specific recall, how then shall one forgive? As I mentioned above, the "ease" of forgiveness is dependant, in part, upon the depth and extent of the suffering the offence has brought on. In Scripture we find stories, teaching, and dramatic events which relate to this challenge of forgiving offences which are either virtually innumerable, or profoundly serious.

In the context of Jesus' teaching about sin and relationships (Matthew 18), Peter asked the Master about the practice of forgiveness: "How often shall my brother sin against me and I forgive him?" (v. 21). In possibly trying to outdo the rabbis of the time, Peter goes beyond their limit— set at three or four—and wonders if seven acts of forgiveness would do it. In his response, Jesus blew away all such limits: "Not seven times, but, I tell you, seventy-seven times" (v. 22, NRSV).

The impossibility of such shocking generosity should be clear to anyone who has nursed any sort of grudge for a grievance suffered, a wrong done, a right deprived. The wrongs I have in mind here are not trivial items which may almost have escaped notice if someone had not brought them to your attention, but rather, serious offences, cutting insults, vicious crimes, weighty debts. And the directive given by Jesus is that of unlimited release of *all* obligations and offences suffered.

Jesus adds an explanatory story, which if anything places this generosity of spirit on the level of the equally uncommon heights of human society. It's a story of a king, his apparent viceroy—a servant — and another of the king's servants. The first servant in question ends up owing the king a colossal sum of money, described in the text as "ten thousand talents" (v. 24). The following graphic explanation puts this sum in far more understandable terms, as Matthew's readers no doubt already understood:

> *The incredible figure of ten thousand talents would represent the total revenue of a wealthy province.... [The] taxes paid in a year by Judea, Idumaca, Samaria, Galilee, and Perea amounted to only 800 talents. It cannot be thought of as a loan, a debt which the "slave" has incurred. We must think rather of him as the satrap of a great province of the Persian Empire, let us say, who*

*has diverted to his own use vast sums that should have
been sent on to the imperial treasure* (Beare, 382).

This is no trifling sum! But when the king ordered the
man and his family to be sold and the debt repaid, the man
begged for mercy—and time to repay! In an act of incredible
royal generosity, the king forgave the man, releasing him of his
debt. Beare further notes, "A Sultan, or a Caliph, or an Indian
prince would be capable of as much extravagance in grace as
in cruelty"(p. 382).

But this man, newly released from his incredible debt,
came across another fellow servant who owed him "a hundred
denarii" (v. 28) —about three to four months' wages for a
casual laborer. At the level of financial activity at which these
servants seemed to be accustomed, this amount would likely
be significant enough to notice, but not overwhelming. The
man demands payment, but upon receiving nothing but a plea
for patience and time—echoes of his own words!—he tosses
the offender into jail until all is paid.

The story ends with the king hearing of his servant's
cruelty, and in anger, handing him over to be tortured until he
has paid his own debt, asking the question, "Should you not
also have had mercy on your fellow slave, even as I had mercy
on you?" (v. 33). Perhaps the slave knew where the money
was, and the king knew that pain would reveal its
whereabouts; it is not apparent in the tale as it was told.

What *is* apparent is the amazing freedom with which
forgiveness is expected. Jesus concludes his response to Peter's
question by picking up on the king's reaction to his
unforgiving servant: "So shall My heavenly Father also do to
you, if each of you does not forgive his brother from your
heart" (v. 35). A parallel has been drawn here between the

king, his servant, God and ourselves. The model of forgiveness for us is the incredible generosity of the king, who released his servant from an unbelievable debt. The king also models the unyielding expectation of mercy which God has: We are *required* to forgive.

Implicit in this story is a stark contrast between what we owe the King, and what others owe us. We owe God a staggering amount. What others owe us is significant, but not overwhelming. We may *feel* that the injustice we've suffered is overwhelming, but this story completely changes our perspective by highlighting the vast disparity between what others owe us, and our own indebtedness towards God.

We owe the "King" more than we are capable of understanding. We live and participate in darkness, and the darkness has permeated our every thought and action and motive and intent. Only those who have traveled a long way towards the light can begin to understand how dark is our darkness. For those at the very beginning of this journey, although they may see some outstanding areas of wrong in their own lives, the thoroughness of their state will only become apparent as time moves on, as they draw ever nearer to God, as they walk ever further along the way of his commands.

Somehow in moving through this passage on forgiveness, God has again taken center stage. Just as marriage itself is "not about me," so forgiveness is also not about me. Forgiveness has to do with our relationship with God. God is the model of mercy, of granting unmerited favor. It is also he who requires of us equal generosity of heart when forgiving one another: "We love, because He first loved us" (1 John 4:19).

Does all of this make forgiveness any easier? I think it does, because it places the offender and the offended in a relational context with God. At the center of my deprivation, pain, suffering and grievance is not that other person, that group of people, or even my spouse—but God. Although the love, respect, justice and fairness which others owe me is truly significant in itself, this is virtually nothing in comparison with my debt towards God.

The suffering aspect of forgiveness brings to mind two events found in Scripture in which we see forgiveness modeled. These are similar to the teaching about mercy seen above; they demonstrate mercy in the midst of intense suffering. All of this places our relationship with our spouse in a much larger setting; a setting which has God at its center.

ADDING INSULT TO INJURY

Many of us suffer because of folly — either our own, or that of others. Aside from this—which likely happens far more than we realize!—we may on occasion actually suffer from "righteousness." In a mild form, this may arise because the good that we have done, or intended to do, has been completely misunderstood. Beyond this, though, active opposition solely because of our alignment with God is, in most Western countries, rare. The persecution for righteousness' sake is an extreme form of suffering, in which "the enemy," ourselves and God are placed in clear relationship.

In a marriage relationship, things seldom get so extreme. Even though spouses often invoke a plea of innocence, and the other is assumed solely guilty, the saying has some merit that "it takes two to tangle." But even for marriage, a look at the extreme cases can help to encourage and place in context our own task of working through the necessity of forgiveness.

The generosity of a forgiving spirit in completely unjust situations is well illustrated in Scripture by Stephen, the first Christian martyr, and by Christ himself. A moment's reflection on both situations may help to give some perspective on our usually less dramatic struggles. It may, once again, move our preoccupation with our own concerns off of center stage, and help us to see our situations more clearly in relation to God.

Stephen appears only briefly in Scripture (see Acts 6-7), where he heads the list of those chosen to defuse a difficult and potentially divisive situation. He was chosen to help in the fair distribution of food for widows of both "foreign" and native Jews alike in the initial dynamic and tumultuous days of the early church. Stephen is described as being "full of faith and of the Holy Spirit" (6:5). More than this, he is depicted as "performing great wonders and signs among the people" (v. 8), and refuting those arguing against him with such wisdom and Spirit that they couldn't cope (vv. 9-10)!

When those who had been opposing Stephen saw that they were getting nowhere, they stirred up the people and put forward false witnesses against him before the council. In response to this, and in defense of himself, Stephen gave a rather long-winded historical recounting (Acts 7:2-50!) of God's dealings with Israel. Although he highlighted some of the times Israel had resisted God, it's not until the very end of his "sermon" (vv. 51-53) that he suddenly turns to blast those before him, accusing them of being just like their fathers; for not only did their fathers resist the Holy Spirit, killing the prophets who announced the coming of Christ, but now they themselves have betrayed and murdered the long-awaited Messiah. Harsh news!!

Not surprisingly, this charge enraged his listeners; but they lost it completely when Stephen—gazing into heaven—said, "Look . . . I see the heavens opened and the Son of Man standing at the right hand of God!" (v. 56, NRSV). Upon hearing this, they covered their ears and rushed upon him with a loud shout, dragging him out of the city to stone him. As Stephen was dying, having already asked the Lord Jesus to receive his spirit, his last recorded words were, "Lord, do not hold this sin against them" (v. 60).

It takes a considerable degree of spiritual maturity and insight not to take this sort of opposition personally! Stephen was really clear about the spiritual dynamics which were going on. Although many, many Jews had already accepted the gospel message, some were in decided opposition. As Jesus had done while on earth (Matthew 23:13-39), and as the prophets had done throughout history, such opposition was pointed out and condemned clearly as being opposition to the purpose and activity of God. Stephen's death came about because of his allegiance to God. In his last dying moments, Stephen displayed the same generous spirit of forgiveness which all Christians are to have to anyone who has done them wrong.

Jesus said something similar while on the cross, in keeping with his earlier teaching: "Love your enemies ... pray for those who mistreat you" (Luke 6:27-28). Having been beaten, mocked, unfairly and falsely accused, and unjustly condemned to death by hanging on a cross, Jesus exemplified the heart of God's mercy by praying, "Father, forgive them; for they do not know what they are doing" (Luke 23:34).

Jesus—declared innocent by Pilate, sinless by all subsequent Christians, indeed a righteous sufferer like no other—this One forgave all those who did him wrong. Indeed, he had said earlier that all sins against "the Son of Man" would be forgiven, but the sin against the Holy Spirit would never be forgiven (see Matthew 12:24-32). In saying this, Jesus clearly distinguished between all those who had sinned against him personally in whatever way, and those who opposed the source of Jesus' power and authority: the Spirit of God. This opposition was the blasphemy of the Pharisees, who preferred to believe that the spiritual power source of Jesus' remarkable ministry was "the ruler of the demons" (v. 24), rather than admit that Jesus was from God (see also Matthew 21:23-27).

Jesus, the "author and perfecter" of our faith (Hebrews 12:2), and Stephen, the first Christian martyr, demonstrated in their final hour an almost unbelievable spirit of forgiveness. In contrast to these two extreme situations, most of what we need to forgive within our marriages is much milder. The admonition to freely forgive one's spouse can take on a different weight when seen in this light.

But All Is Not Darkness

These two accounts of such generous forgiveness do not make light of any serious offence, cutting insult, vicious crime or weighty debt we may have suffered because of our spouse. In directing us to the unlimited release of *all* obligations owing and offences suffered, Jesus knew what lay in store for himself.

Since his birth, he had suffered persecution, and at the very beginning of his public ministry he had a prolonged encounter with the devil (Luke 4:1 -13). But in all of this he suffered innocently; that is, he deserved none of it whatsoever. We, on the other hand, are not guiltless in every respect.

There is no doubt we do suffer undeservedly; the folly, greed, neglect or sheer ignorance of others can cause or increase our suffering considerably. But apart from this, what we get and what we deserve are sometimes quite unrelated. This can work to our advantage.

God "makes his sun rise on the evil and on the good, and sends rain on the righteous and on the unrighteous" (Matthew 5:45, NRSV). All people, whether good or bad, enjoy many of God's blessings in many aspects of life: family, marriage, friends, communities, provisions, times of peace and prosperity. Moreover, God is habitually slow in executing judgment, patiently waiting, "not wishing for any to perish but for all to come to repentance" (2 Peter 3:9).

Beyond this, there is our natural relationship with God. For each person, often regarded as "good" or "bad," Scripture says that ultimately "there is none righteous, not even one" (Romans 3:10). *We* belong on the cross, not Christ. As one of the thieves who was crucified alongside of Jesus said to the other, when he rebuked him for mocking Jesus, "Do you not fear God, since you are under the same sentence of condemnation? And we indeed have been condemned justly, for we are getting what we deserve for our deeds, but this man has done nothing wrong" (Luke 23:40–41, NRSV).

I deserve more suffering than I receive, and I do not deserve the goodness which is present every day in my life— regardless of how little I may be aware of it! I do not deserve the good my wife does, and is, for me. The good that we receive through creation, and through others, is an aspect of the goodness of God's open-hearted generosity to all. The fact that I do not suffer according to the folly I have pursued, the darkness I still cling to, the rebellion I grasp after, is due to the overwhelming patience of the Father who waits for his wayward one to fully come home.

Granting forgiveness can be exceedingly challenging indeed. We are not innocent sufferers; we suffer in part because of our own inadequacies and errors. But not only do we *not* suffer as we rightly or fully deserve, we are, moreover, undeservedly blessed. Somehow, in view of these things, our difficult and weighty grievances can become lighter. As we grow deeper into the spirit of "a broken and a contrite heart" (Psalm 51:17) for the hardships we *do* deserve, and as we progress in developing a heart of gratitude for the good which we do *not* deserve, the necessity for exercising forgiveness—even towards our spouse—can become a lighter yoke to carry.

ALWAYS A STEP FURTHER

After forgiveness has been requested and given, then what? Both spouses need to accept that change has taken place, and that further change is on the way. But the request for forgiveness and the granting of it are deficient, without a doubt! Have I truly repented? Am I really determined—by the grace of God—to change? Did I secretly enjoy that brief moment when I blew off some steam; do I really care that my spouse was hurt by it all? On the other side of it, do I bear a grudge? Have I really let the other off? Have I released the requirements of obligation and put this infraction behind me?

A whole range of emotions and states can accompany this entire procedure. There's emotional and sometimes physical pain, deprivation of all types, fear and frustration. All the things which can arise in the inner life of a person may become entwined in the messiness of relationships where forgiveness is needed. This is why it is so helpful to regard repentance, and forgiveness, as both a moment and a way of life. It takes a moment to drop a pot of stew; it can take much longer to clean up the mess from the table, the floor, and even from one's clothing. The sin of a moment can leave a stain for a lifetime. This can affect our "inner person" as well as our relationships, although the grace of God can work effectively in the life of a believer: "The blood of Jesus . . . cleanses us from all sin" (1 John 1:7).

The mind-set and the heart, the posture and the commitment which are implicit in these three little words— "Please, forgive me"—can make such a radical change in any relationship. How much more will the practice of obedience in this area radically transform marriage! This is constantly the challenge and yet the hope which confronts us: blessed are those who hear the word of God, and do it (Luke 11:28; Marshall, 482). This is the journey from silence, to confession.

Biblical Illustrations and Teaching

1. In Psalm 51:4, the psalmist prays to God, "Against you, you alone, have I sinned" (NRSV). In a similar way, the Prodigal Son said to his father, "Father, I have sinned

against heaven and before you" (Luke 15:21, NRSV). What is the effect of moving God front and center into the midst of our grievances; of seeing all offences against ourselves as being, more fundamentally, against God?

2. At the beginning of this chapter, I began with a portion of Ephesians 4:32, which in its entirety reads, "And be kind to one another, tender-hearted, forgiving each other, just as God in Christ also has forgiven you." Do these words describe your marriage relationship? If not, what things need to change?

3. In their calls to repentance, John the Baptist and Paul the apostle spoke of the need to "bear fruits worthy of repentance" (Luke 3:8, NRSV), and to "do deeds consistent with repentance" (Acts 26:20, NRSV). What specific changes are you working on (in thought, word, or deed) to make true your repentance(s)?

Little Exercises

1. Read Galatians 5:22-23, on how the Spirit affects our character and relationships over the course of a lifetime. Consider each item and see how you measure up in your marriage. Confess to God where you are deficient or resistant to display any "fruit," praying with, and for, one another in this regard.

2. Are there any unresolved grievances between you and your spouse? If you can't think of any, pray about it, and try asking your spouse (make sure you're open to hearing!) or a close friend who knows you both. What sins do you

need to confess and forsake — either the "doing" kind, or the things you should have done but haven't?

3. Reflect upon and give thanks for the good in your spouse which you do not deserve. Tell him/her about these praiseworthy things (see Philippians 4:8)!

Chapter 3

CLONES & COMPANIONS

The Journey from Maze to Mystery

But for Adam no suitable helper was found.
Genesis 2:20, NIV

*"She's a very nice, attractive Christian girl. What more
could I ask for?"*
*"You know, I have to think hard to remember what I saw
in him!"*
*"I'm twenty-three; if I don't say yes to him, who else will
ask?"*
*"My wife? We don't do much together. She does her thing,
I do my thing."*
*"We're just not compatible; why should anybody put up
with that?"*

Relationships can be so chaotic and confusing; and in the
midst of it all, we never stop searching for clarity. Whether a
relationship is developing or it's a "done deal," the same
questions arise. What is it that makes for a good match?
What am I to make of our differences?

"Opposites attract." Sure — why marry a mirror?
But opposites repel, too, don't they? (Do I hear
cries of, "You betcha!" in the background; with
humor, with despair?)
"Birds of a feather flock together." Does that go for
mates as well? Shouldn't we have similar goals
and values? Or is too much sameness simply
boring?
"The good Lord that made 'em, matched 'em."
Spoken about couples who seemed to "deserve"
each other, in a bad sort of way. I've also heard
it used about couples who need to work out their
***own** self-inflicted problems.*

On this last somewhat pathological note, consider the following brilliantly-worded confession on what typically draws out the worst in us:

Couples choose each other with an unerring instinct for
finding the very person who will exactly match their own
level of unconscious anxieties and mirror their own
dysfunctions, and who will trigger for them all their
unresolved emotional pain (Maté, 32).

I can just hear a marriage counselor, after discussing the possibility of a couple's marriage, saying, "You two seem dysfunctionally well suited—go for it!"

These sayings and comments highlight only some of the positive and negative things which may draw a couple together. This is assuming that they are being drawn from *within*, as opposed to being put together by purely external forces (like family pressures, an unwanted pregnancy, or even a prearranged marriage). There are countless influences which may affect the true marriage, the real connectedness, of a couple. We are such complex creatures, and we come up with so many explanations and ideas to explain what goes on in relationships.

This quest for understanding "the other" is a ongoing enterprise. Catherine Johnson, a contributing editor to *New Woman* magazine, mentioned in a book on relationships and the brain:

> *A fair amount of women's magazine time and energy, it must be said, goes into trying to figure out why men do the things they do (Ratey & Johnson, 30).*

In thinking about the hows and whys of relationships and marriage, we will first take time out to consider that our minds should boggle over *all* of life's complexities—and not just those of relationships. This is a journey in itself, and an important one. Life isn't simply a maze, it is amazing. If we don't grasp the wonder of this truth—and allow ourselves to be grasped by it—we'll either settle for some simplistic view of people and relationships, or we might get hopelessly lost in the never-ending maze of ideas and explanations which constantly bombard us from every side.

From this humbling context of the 'maze' of life, we can then move on to mystery; to perspectives and insights about how "fitting together" can take place in our own relationships. First, the maze.

CURIOUS DIFFERENCES

The other day, my young son brought home a book on ants. As we started the walk home from the school bus, he began to tell me with great enthusiasm all about ants. I was amazed to hear about all sorts of ants I'd never dreamed existed. Moreover, the book stated that there are over 9,000 kinds of ants in the world. Wow!

I am impressed with such diversity among what appears to be a unified group of insects — they're all ants!

I am even more amazed with those enthusiasts and scientists who spent years classifying such minute differences. What curious creatures we people are, endlessly fascinated and ever seeking to understand the world in which we live. God evidently delights in diversity in all his created works, and we in turn spend a considerable amount of energy trying to understand what he has done.

People have, if anything, put even more time and effort into understanding other people. This has resulted in a staggering amount of accumulated ideas, insights and wisdom about people and about relationships.

I have on my shelves a recent book explaining over one hundred different ways of explaining different types of people. These are ways which have been explored and expanded upon within many cultures and throughout many ages. And all of this has been done in the context of many religions and in a vast variety of social settings.

The author of this wide-ranging collection takes an open-ended approach to these various models, seeing none of them as perfect or complete, but only suggestive. His advice is to try on all approaches and see what fits. In the end he appears to see the individual as being greater than even all such models added together (Godwin, Introduction). This would certainly be my own approach; each individual is far greater than any one system which attempts to explain him or her. Each scheme naturally focuses on some things and not others. Any notion which attempts to describe the differences and similarities of people is naturally limited and incomplete.

If it is so difficult to understand even one individual, how then can we hope to comprehend how two might make sense as a couple? The differences between individuals make for an infinite number of possible connections and conflicts once they are in relationship with others.

These differences can become really obvious in the constant challenge of communication, as psychiatrist Andrew Abarbanel pointed out:

> *Human communication, it seems to me, is implausible in the best of circumstances. People are wildly different in their psychological issues, quirks, and hang-ups, in their benign or traumatic experiences growing up, in their personality styles, intellectual styles, cultural backgrounds, interests, talents, preferences, and on and on ...Even Freud... thought that without the bond of sexual attraction, men and women would have long since exterminated one another* (11-12).

In the light of such diversity among individuals, how can anyone know how any two people might make it as a couple? The models and ideas people have come up with are usually explained in a few simple terms, but how can such simplicity capture all the complexity of human relationships?

SELF-MULTIPLYING MAZES

Using the accumulated wisdom of humanity to explore relationships is like taking a small flashlight in hand to explore a large underground cave full of intricate passageways. The light of humanity's wisdom is in itself an endless maze. It not only tries to comprehend both the visible and invisible complexities of God's created works, but the mind itself generates endless explanations and insights.

In this day, not only can we not comprehend the whole of life, we cannot even comprehend thin slices of it. Our world is overflowing with specialists, and every field of specialization seems to only create even more areas of specialization. Even specialists in the same general area of study hardly know the fine print of what those in the next room are studying.

This situation was commented on humorously by John Gribbin, as he reflected on his thirty years of explaining science on a popular level:

> *The fate of specialists in any area of science is to focus more and more narrowly on their special topic, learning more and more about less and less, until eventually they end up knowing everything about nothing.*
>
> *It was in order to avoid such a fate that, many years ago, I chose to become a writer about science, rather than a researcher. The opportunity this gave me to question real scientists about their work, and to report my findings in a series of books and articles, enabled me to learn less and less about more and more, although as yet I have not*

quite reached the stage of knowing nothing about everything (1).

It is not only science which is overrun with multiple and multiplying fields of specialties. When I went off to seminary some twenty years ago, I was introduced to some of the approaches used in biblical studies. This included things I'd never heard of before, all trying to understand how the different parts of Scripture were written up and eventually put together. Yet these approaches are considered old—as in "traditional"—in biblical studies. Newer approaches include even more unusual things like structuralism, reader-response, narrative, feminist and poststructuralist criticism (McKenzie and Haynes). Who would guess that the study of Scripture is so complicated? But the study of it is as easily diversified as the field of medicine, which, as we know, is filled with all kinds of specialists!

And as I turned to the area of trying to help people through counseling, I was once again confronted with an incredible variety and number of theories and psychotherapies. Roger Hurding, after discussing the main schools of counseling of the last two centuries, lists over fifteen *new* therapies, before focusing on (only!) four of these for his extended discussion (180-181). Another writer in the mid-1970s, referring to an earlier work which outlined thirty-six systems, estimated that in the fifteen years following, "at least double that number of counseling approaches could be identified" (Crabb, *Basic Principles,* 21). So much for a quick-and-easy method for offering help!

The more we study and analyze any part of God's creation, the more we are confronted with the overwhelming complexity of the world, and of ourselves. Regarding relationships, what approach can we depend on? When these questions arise ("Is he the one for me? Do we make sense together?"), what explanation, what understanding of people, can we trust?

PEBBLES ON THE BEACH

Many people believe that wisdom is to be found through education, and that salvation (from a variety of ills) will come through our scientific cleverness. With the fantastic increase of knowledge, and in the present new age of information, it can be easy to think that we can come to understand everything.

On the other hand, many thinkers at the end of the twentieth century—while admitting the brilliant benefits that science has brought—increasingly stress the limited nature of scientific models and explanations. If this is true of the "hard" sciences that explore the physical universe, how much more so is it of the "soft" sciences that attempt to understand human society at both the individual and the collective level?

The apple falling on the head of Sir Isaac Newton may well have been the singular innocent event which redirected his thinking and led to his discovery of gravity. However it came about, Newton's explanation of the universe held sway for two centuries! What a lucky man! The great philosopher Spinoza said, "Newton was a most fortunate man, for God only made one universe, and Newton discovered its laws." But Newton, who was also the first scientist to be knighted by the Queen, spoke more modestly about himself and his work:

I do not know what I may appear to the world; but to myself I seem to have been only a boy, playing on the

*seashore, and diverting myself now and then finding a
smoother pebble or a prettier shell than ordinary, while
the great ocean of truth lay all undiscovered before me
(Hutchings, 183).*

The accumulated wisdom of humanity is like the pebbles
at the seashore; yet life's complexities, like the vast ocean, still
lie before us, mocking our best efforts to comprehend it all.
This means that, for any one person, we're not as smart as we
sometimes like to pretend we are.   But are we really
convinced?

For those still unconverted, whose minds refuse to boggle,
who think they can figure it all out, let's pause a moment
further and see how limited our reasoning is. Those of you
who are convinced can skip ahead to the next section!

Borrowing insights from the realm of science is useful
here, since many of us almost instinctively regard science and
math as dealing with hard little bits of truth, or data, and their
"laws" as being determinative. On the other hand, the study
of people and humanity is considered a "soft" science—more
open to subjective interpretation.

Referring again to Gribbin's work, *Almost Everyone's Guide
to Science*, it is noteworthy that he spends almost half of his
introductory comments explaining the limited nature of
scientific models. Illustrating his discussion with some models
used by scientists to describe the air that we breathe (arguably
fairly common stuff), he concludes with the following
comment:

*None of the models is the ultimate Deep Truth, but they
all have their part to play. They are tools which we use
to help our imaginations to get a picture of what is going*

on, and to calculate things which we can test....Just as a carpenter would not use a chisel to do the same job as a mallet, so a scientist must chose the right model for the job in hand....

[Even] the best model is only a good one in its own context, and ... chisels should never be used to do the job of mallets. Whenever we describe something as being "real," what we mean is that it is the best model to use in the relevant circumstances (6-7).

Another writer who has attempted to bring into focus the "total universe" is Todd Siler, in his book, *Breaking the Mind Barrier.* As the first visual artist to receive a doctorate from MIT, Siler attempts in his book to show how both science and art reflect the same human mind grappling with the same universe. Like Gribbin, he clarifies the limited nature of scientific understanding in his introductory comments:

We begin with what the fifteenth-century theologian, mathematician, and statesman Cardinal Nicholas of Cusa called "learned ignorance." We start from that humble point and shortly thereafter conclude: There are definitive truths — but only in limited frames of reference. We are privileged with modest insights which we use to illuminate nature. The discovery and interpretation of facts and truths depend on the exploratory perspective, beliefs, contexts, assumptions, and unique prejudices of the interpreter. There's just no way around this reality.

[We] may ultimately never understand ourselves in a strictly biological or physical sense...this knowledge may

*continually escape us as we try to grasp the modeler's place
or part in the models of nature (23).*

Where do we then go, if reason is so limited? Where is
wisdom to be found?

REPHRASING THE QUEST

Perhaps the question, "Where can I find *the* Answer?"
should be rephrased, "What am I supposed to do with the
answers we've found?" We need to move from the
question, "Where is wisdom to be found?" to the question,
"Where is wisdom to be placed?" We have seen how the
creation of God is mysterious beyond our comprehension. In
our attempts to explain the intricacies of our world, people
and relationships, we are unable to discover any one picture
which encompasses all things. What we come up with,
instead, are insights containing partial truths.

I began this chapter with the question, "In the midst of
[mystery] ... we seek clarity: What is it that makes for a good
match?" From what has been said above, there is no one all-
encompassing answer. What we find is not "The Answer," but
many "answers." The mind can only help us so far.

This is not to say that we should stop using our brains—
especially with respect to something as involved and intricate
as relationships and marriage. After all, we have to live with
our decisions, and with whatever happens in our closer
relationships. We could only *stop* thinking about such things
by a tremendous act of the will, but Scripture does not lead us
to such unnatural extremes. In the main biblical book which
reflects the cumulative wisdom of Israel, we find a strongly-
stated perspective on where all wisdom is to be placed.

Big Ocean - Little Sail

While we were living in Hong Kong, we frequently took a "tea break" at a spot overlooking the harbor. As I watched the numerous boats and ships coming and going, I reflected how this dynamic picture is an apt portrait of how wisdom is set forth in the Old Testament book of Proverbs.

Gaining wisdom, understanding, insight, etc., can be likened to the learning of the craft of sailing. You can learn all that can be known about ropes and sails and winds and tides; but in the end, you climb aboard and—with a prayer in your heart—cast off.

In the introductory verses of Proverbs there is a nautical "skill" term used in the description of what one can gain by wisdom. This means that Proverbs 1:5 can be rendered as "the discerning *learn the ropes*" (McKane, 76). But the goal of learning the ropes is not to merely learn the ropes; one takes time to acquire life skills in order to then move back into the regular stream of life and use them.

Proverbs relates wisdom to faith. It shows us how we need to relate all our ideas about people and relationships to our trust in God. The following excerpt brings much of this to light:

> *Trust in the LORD with all your heart,*
> *And do not lean on your own understanding.*
> *In all your ways acknowledge Him,*
> *And He will make your paths straight.*
> *Do not be wise in your own eyes;*
> *Fear the LORD and turn away from evil*
> (3:5-7).

In these verses—possibly the best known from Proverbs—wholehearted trust in God is set in contrast to depending on our own understanding. This is not a put-down of learning, for Proverbs exhorts us strongly to get all the wisdom we can:

The beginning of wisdom is: Acquire wisdom;
And with all your acquiring, get understanding
(4:7).

Wisdom, understanding, insight and knowledge are all worthwhile, commendable and helpful, and they're promised to all who desire them in the preface of Proverbs (1:2-6). Models, ideas, books, seminars and discussion groups on marriage, relationships and people are great. There is no place in Proverbs for not using our thinking faculties; taking thought is strongly commended!

The hundreds of proverbs listed from Proverbs 10 and onward are evidence that we are supposed to use our "grey matter," that is, our brains! Indeed, portions of Proverbs—especially in the first nine chapters—seem to "promise the moon" for those who gain wisdom. With the gaining of wisdom, one also stands to gain long life, peace, blessedness, security and more (3:13–26)!

The issue in Proverbs 3:5-7 is not about whether you should or should not use your brains, or wisdom. The issue is rather one of reliance. In the final analysis, when push comes to shove and decisions need to be made, which will we trust—our own insight and discernment, or God?

In a world reeling with innumerable "prophets" and "seers," degrees, studies and experts without end, it is a strong temptation to rely on the latest glamorous trend, book, author or speaker for insight and guidance. After all, what can I, as a lone individual, know? We are reliant upon each other for many, perhaps most, aspects of life, so we look to "those who know" for guidance. But *all* such wisdom, from the worldly or the religious, can never supplant our ever basic need of relating and submitting all things—even our highest and best—to God.

All wisdom and understanding find their proper place in the context of trust, of faith. This is shown by the key maxim of Proverbs, the "fear of the Lord." The tone for the entire book is set by the placement of this phrase in two strategically situated verses. They state that the fear of the Lord is "the beginning of knowledge" (1:7) and "the beginning of wisdom" (9:10).

"The fear of the Lord" is a catchall expression that gathers up all of the ways in which Old Testament believers were to trust and obey the Lord their God. This view of learning and wisdom set forth in Proverbs is profoundly religious. Our best efforts to understand—as worthwhile, commendable and helpful as they may be—are second to the most crucial and foundational of relationships; to the life of trust in, and obedience to, God.

This means that *the life of faith is the foundational and necessary context for understanding your mate.* This is also true for trying to figure out who makes sense as a possible mate. This "life of faith" is not, of course, merely something done in your head—like agreeing to some mathematical axiom. The "fear of the Lord" in the Old Testament, like the term "faith" in the New Testament, is a total life response to God; a response in which one is committed to, and grows toward, complete trust and thorough obedience.

Wisdom, understanding, insight and knowledge are all limited; worthwhile, commendable and at times helpful, but limited. The hundreds of proverbs found in the book of Proverbs are a useful collection of insights. They are much like the hundreds of theories and models used in counseling or biblical studies or science; they all have their place in the greater scheme of things. But even the appropriate understanding and use of such things requires wisdom. According to Proverbs, that ability, with respect to understanding people and relationships, needs to find its place in the context of a life submitted, above all, to God.

All the relational skills and people know-how are only a thumbnail sketch of what lies ahead on the seas of matrimony. In the complexity of God's created works we find mystery. In our desire to understand his works, the life of faith must be preeminent, especially when it comes to understanding ourselves and others. And knowing someone, understanding him or her, is not something that can simply be done in your head. It must be done in the context of relationship — the foundational relationship with God, and in being in relationship with the other person. In that context, wisdom can speak.

In the absence of God, dependence upon wisdom can lead to despair; for we cannot, by ourselves, unravel and comprehend all of life's intricacies—although we keep trying!

But in the presence of God, wisdom can lead us to wonder, amazement and praise of the Creator whose ways and works are beyond our comprehension.

Building upon the bedrock of faith, we don't need to despair about the maze of life's complexities and humanity's countless explanations. We face the same reality; but the endless maze becomes an intriguing mystery. We don't need to know "The Answer." Instead, we can walk with the One who is the source of all answers. In this faith, we can relax as we trust our cares and questions to God. And in hope, we can grow into an ever-deepening comprehension of the mystery of people and relationships.

Faith, Feeling and Logic

Some people live by their heads, others by their hearts. For better or worse, I seem about evenly split between the two. I was extremely shocked in my counseling courses to discover that I'm as feeling and intuitive as I am analytical. In the end, however, neither intuition nor rational analysis merits complete trust; both have their place, but neither are absolute.

The mind may say, "I see clearly the snow on yonder mountain peaks," whereas intuition may fill in a picture beyond the visible and apparent ("I have a feeling that there are some really lush green valleys beyond those bright mountain peaks"). Things seen and things "felt" are a part of how we perceive and understand the world, including people and relationships; but we must ultimately rely, once again, on God himself.

The opening quote at the beginning of this chapter came from my own experience. After going with a girl for over two years, I thought to myself, "She's a very nice, attractive Christian girl. What more could I ask for?" The point was, it wasn't enough—but I couldn't figure out why. Things looked good, we "made sense" together, but it just didn't feel right. That inner, intuitive, "Yes! She's the one!" wasn't coming like I expected it to. We agreed to pray for a few weeks while I was away on vacation and ask whether or not we should carry on. Notice that the answer that came, the "wisdom" or insight I eventually received, came about in that context of relationships, with God, and with others.

The answer struck me as I was reading the same passage which I also placed at the start of this chapter — the suitability of Eve for Adam. Unlike those two, we two just "didn't fit." Instead of our combined strengths becoming stronger, ours clashed and couldn't develop. Instead of our weaknesses or deficiencies being automatically shored up by the other, our weaknesses overlapped. Now I look back and realize, "Great friends, lousy mates."

With that new insight, I, and we, could then see clearly enough to say the difficult "no" to continuing our relationship. We parted with tears and well wishes. That moment of "rational clarity" made the next step clear for that one relationship. I headed off into the unknown; but with this experience, as is often the case, something of enduring worth had been learned.

In the forming of Eve as finally someone suitable, someone who corresponded to Adam, we can see something of an example for every marriage. Marriage makes the most sense when there is a counterbalancing, a suitability, a fitting together which exists between two individuals.

The ways in which two may fit together are both complex and fluid, for people are complex beings and none of us remain static in the development of what distinguishes our character and personality. Despite this, more counterbalance is preferable to less, at least in areas that are central to one's unique strengths and gifts.

How does the understanding of counterbalance help in trying to figure out if any particular two are a good match? The realization that "opposites" (or better, "complements") "attract" can help one to look for and see suitability more clearly. All the numerous and complicated ways which humanity has devised for understanding people *may* help to highlight how two fit together. Even though such insight is limited, that insight may be just the one clue—or, more likely, one of a few—we need to see the potential goodness of a certain relationship.

I personally think that some simple guidelines — not in isolation from life, but as expressed in the context of relationships (friends, family, or community) — will point more readily to possible suitability. More readily, that is, than 101 complex models, which most of us would find more than just a little overwhelming. But before I consider community and couples, I want to consider how the awareness and acceptance—or not!—of suitability affects marriages which already exist.

A Steady Spark?

One of the ways in which I have seen the potential usefulness of understanding counterbalancing has been with couples who are married, but are unwilling to let the other function effectively, or develop uniquely. Usually this seems to develop because of a variety of factors which can suppress the expression, use and development of one's innate strengths and abilities.

Many things can choke off the growth and contribution of a spouse. Grasping after, or being consumed by, the development of one's own potential can negate the other's. Defining a person's contribution to a marriage primarily in terms of social or cultural expectations, but without regard for the individual's own implicit areas of strength, can also war against the development of a person as a unique being. Even just an obstinate unwillingness, or perhaps a complete inability, to see and nurture the other's potential may stunt their growth.

For my wife, being spontaneous adds spark to life and is *fun*! As often happens in couples, her long-suffering spouse thinks that being *routine* is fun, because then he can finally get some work done! This may sound boring, but I happen to love my various pursuits, and I find dreaming up and completing goals is (dare I say it) *fun*! Can you see any potential conflict in this scenario?

If I insisted on plodding after my long-term goals at the expense of my wife's short-term "let's take a break and do something completely out of the ordinary" intrusions, the spark in her would die. If she insisted in living a totally spontaneous life, in which I could never plot out and follow my somewhat idiosyncratic quests, something in me would also die. We would both lose something that we cherish and enjoy about the other, and we would also lose out in not having a natural "deficiency" counterbalanced. I need her to minister to me by taking the unexpected break, by doing out-of-routine things just for the fun of doing them. She needs me to minister to her by establishing routines that are important. In giving way to the other, we gain.

In this one area of life — a pretty important one for us — we benefit by allowing the other person to "make us" do what we would not naturally be inclined to do. I'm still not spontaneous, but I am better able to roll with spontaneity when it comes. Sarah is still not wild over routine, but she can get in there and make some of the routine necessities of life more fun (and faster, too!).

If I sound like a hero in this, I'm not. A wise supervisor once told me that I needed to build "waste time" (read, "people time") into my life. That was before I met my wife-to-be. So when we did meet and I started to get interested in her, this concept of "waste time" was really clear in my head. I knew what I was getting myself into.

Sarah was, and always will be (I'm sure!), spontaneous, fun-loving and people-oriented. The spontaneous/structured pull between us is probably the most constant area that demands my attention in our marriage. The joy of knowing her does not mean that I simply "put up" with something I would otherwise find unbearable; it means that I deliberately choose to cherish that which I already enjoy about her, even when it conflicts with my natural temperament. To do otherwise would be relational death; to fight it would be worse.

THE ONE-MAN SHOW

When a couple gets married, they become one; and—so the joke goes—they spend the rest of their lives trying to figure out which one! Who is at the center of your relationship? The right and correct "Sunday School" answer may be "God." But is that the reality? Or is it the husband? Is it the wife? Is it his career, or her goals? Perhaps, neither.

George was highly trained in his field and fairly well-situated, job-wise. Unfortunately, his company was young and struggling to find its place in the wider world of commerce. As a result, everybody had to work extra hours, while at the same time accepting a lower-than-average salary.

Meanwhile, George's wife, an incredibly capable and multi-talented woman, moved into a number of jobs seeking to supplement their income. All would be well with this situation, except that George could not live with the thought that his wife earned more than he did! The outcome was that George's wife passed up offers of promotion, and stayed away from jobs in which she might have developed and ended up earning more than her husband.

I put the title *The One-Man Show* on this section because it's often the man (but certainly not always!) who does not, or cannot, see how he obliterates his wife just by "being himself"—either the person he is unthinkingly, or the man he feels he "ought" to be. This can play itself out in a number of ways, for there are many areas in which a couple may have relative strengths that complement relative weaknesses (deficiencies, lesser abilities) in each other.

Money and income can become a part of this dynamic. From time to time, my father would remark about how expensive something was. If I were so ignorant as to say, "Wow, that's worth a lot!" he would immediately remind me of the difference between value and cost. The market determines the cost of something (generally speaking), whereas its value may be much less, or infinitesimally more, than its price. The *cost* of a fun-looking two-seater sports car is often far more than its *value* to a family with four kids.

The same goes for wages and salaries, and even for job availability. People with many degrees in theology (my own area of training) simply aren't highly valued in today's market.

Jobs are scarce in that area. Moreover, the pay in most related positions is far less than one would expect from the years of learning, as compared to many other areas which also entail over a decade of university education. This is simply a reality of our current non-to-anti-Christian society. It is also a reality that exists in many other areas of learning and skills.

So what happens to the male ego when the wife can go out and earn way more than the husband can (a situation which can happen regardless of one's area of training)? This is a topic unto itself! If the wife is naturally a very capable and practical person (which seems a pretty natural "complement" of many academic types), will he allow her to blossom; or will she be held in check because he can't take her "providing for the family"? These questions aren't applicable only to people in my own area, of course; economies the world over are being shaken from traditional job roles and expectations.

It is a challenging thing to redefine one's role; it's worse when the change is forced! If we define our relationships primarily in a functional manner, then such change can be devastating. In today's world of not only equal opportunity, but also vast variations between jobs, some will find the changes in "who can earn what" to be very difficult.

In the pursuit of jobs and careers, who will suffer? Will she suffer? Will he suffer? Is it better to make more money by the one who the market pays more? How does the job relate to personal development? It may be entirely unrelated. On the other hand, a well-paying, or at least secure, job may be killing personal growth and unique contribution. Does she see his potential, or is her sole concern security? Practicality and responsible living are good; but so is growing into the person God made you to be. Effective ministry may be set aside in the name of obtaining a socially determined lifestyle, clothed in the guise of necessity.

Modern life is complex and challenging and brings many changes, but these "modern" changes have been taking place for centuries. Who fixes the house up, does the finances, controls the money, arranges the social gatherings. . .and on we could go. In our world exploding with change and opportunity, it's okay to be different, to have different strengths, abilities, areas of concern and endeavor; these things need not necessarily war against real marriage.

In marriage, there is the opportunity to develop into such depth, and such breadth. There can be that built-in cheering section for you in your spouse, who can acknowledge the wonder and greatness of what you have to contribute and can encourage you to develop into someone you could scarcely hope or dream of being, but who you, indeed, are in seed form. But in order to do this, each spouse must also be willing to acknowledge what he or she can and cannot do very well. Allowing another to be strong can be threatening, unless one can see oneself as having relative strengths and abilities, not only within the marriage, but also within the larger community as well.

Our lives do not need to be a "one-man show" in order to be, or become, our truest self. We become more of a person when we can perceive and acknowledge the glory of another person. Some will want to glory in another's evident abilities because they have no concept of their own worth or contribution. To grow into and admit to one's own significant role in the larger community may take some a very long time, but the journey is important; for in realizing your contribution, you can then become more responsible in what you do and don't do. Others need to avoid believing that their role is crucial, and that the kingdom of God will stumble in some fatal sense if they don't achieve their vision.

All of these can enter into the dynamic of a marriage. You may have such an inflated view of your task (life task or present task) that you believe—in action, if not in words— that it merits the death, so to speak, of your spouse. On the other hand, you may have such a deficient view of yourself that you become a non-person by being consumed by your mate. A more biblical, sane and human approach is to recognize the intrinsic worth and relative abilities of both yourself and your spouse, and to work towards developing *both* of you. This is done not just for the greater good of only yourself, but also for the greater community of which you are (or should be) a part.

A COMPLEMENT IN COMMUNITY

For some people, hell is being alone. For others, hell is— or has been—living with others. The inclination of western cultures has been to prize the individual, often at the expense of the community. On the other hand, a constant area of humor and jokes of some non-western, more community-oriented cultures, has been those infernal, interfering in-laws.

It's hard to know what is worse: living in a world of only one, or living in a world of only two. All things being equal, two *are* "better than one," as the sage said in Ecclesiastes (4:9). And although at times "two's company, three's a crowd," generally speaking, two in a *community* of relationships is far better than two living in complete isolation.

Sometimes we may be tempted to expect our spouse to meet our every need; to not only be a complement to ourselves, but to be our "all in all"—as many, many songs put it. But the circle is not complete with just the two of you. No one person is sufficient for any other one person. Even with mother and child, most moms (I'll refrain from saying *every* mom) like a break during those first months of a newborn's total dependency. It's true that we find, or can find, a balance with respect to the more inner, personal and valued aspects of life in our relationship with our spouses. However, no spouse can be equal to fulfilling our every need, desire and/or wish.

We find our complement in the larger community: in relationships, friends, acquaintances, colleagues, neighbors, etc. With respect to the rest of creation, we are like gods and goddesses of this world, bearing the imprint of the Creator's image, ruling over and creatively working his created handiwork—*together*. Our truest self is found in this context, all of which is an integral part of being in relationship with God himself.

In this setting, we can recognize three things. First, neither spouse is their fullest self solely in the context of marriage. This places my focus on a couple's suitability in the context of the larger community. Although we do find a natural and deep counterbalancing between spouses, this is insufficient in itself for any individual's full development, nor does it fully exhaust what we have to contribute to others. True marriage takes place in the context of a community of task and relationship.

Second, we can give thanks, celebrate, cherish, nurture and develop that unique person who is our spouse in a way that recognizes not only their treasured and irreplaceable role within our marriage, but also their special place and contribution to the larger community.

Some people don't need to hear more praise, either because others are always telling them how wonderful and vital they are, or because they are already a legend in their own mind. People who are blinded by their own glory need to be wonder-struck by the amazing and vital role that others play (yes, even their spouse!), and by the realization that God works his will *despite* our faltering efforts, not because of them.

However, many more need to be encouraged, and perhaps directed, with respect to their own significant role in the lives of others. This may take a concerted effort on the part of those not used to seeing their spouse in this way, but I think that this is an integral part of marriage. Part of the adventure of the journey is to grow together into the grace of Christ as it is manifested and developing in and through the lives of each other.

A third implication of seeing marriage suitability in the matrix of community relationships has to do with compatibility. Are you tempted to say, "We're not compatible"? So, who is? None of us are completely compatible with any other individual. I'm not saying this because of our fallen, sinful nature, but because we are too unique, each one of us, not to require significant give-and-take in marriage. Even the nicest person you've ever met has unique likes and dislikes, favorite pastimes, unconscious quirks and mannerisms, values and enthusiasms, any of which would inevitably clash with your own idiosyncrasies if you lived together in the unavoidably intimate space of marriage.

It takes grace to be married to anybody, even to the most wonderful and incredibly well suited, tailor-made spouse in the world! In moving the center of marriage away from oneself ("it's not about you") and centering it on God as an act of worship (echoes of Chapter One), the focus has changed from selfishly pursuing our own innate desires and plans. The pursuit of any God-given desire or ability needs to be done as a service to God, not as a service to pride or to some "great feeling." Moreover, any "self-development"—however legitimate and proper—needs to be in keeping with the loving and equally enthusiastic development of our spouse.

It is sad, and less than Christian, when any couple separates citing "incompatibility," because they pursued their own goals to the detriment of the relationship. It is better, and more of a service to God and others, to pursue any goals, development, dreams and visions in a manner that values what God values — including the sanctity of marriage. This may sound simplistic ("we need to value what God values" — as if all Scripture is clear at every point regarding this), but we tend to get caught up in the urgency of our own immediate pursuits, and lose perspective of what is both crucial and of lasting significance. It takes faith, and sometimes much prayer, wisdom and discussion, to pursue good ends in a good way; but in so doing, the Kingdom is built more surely, and the results are more likely to be more than merely temporal.

Instead of competition driving you apart, allow your relative strengths and abilities to mold you together. Give yourself to prizing and encouraging the other's strengths and abilities. Allow the other to minister to you by doing well— or helping you to learn—what you don't do well. Realize that your relative differences can make life richer, both for yourselves and for others. Marriage can be such a greenhouse, bringing forth beauty and nurture into the lives of many who enjoy its benefit.

THE LISTENING EAR

Some people seem to have been born to talk; others— fortunately for the first group— seem to have been born to listen. The talkers are always in danger of forgetting to listen; the listeners are in danger of never speaking up. For community to work, just as for relationships to work, both speaking and listening need to take place. This applies to the perception and encouragement of newly forming relationships, as well as to the nurturing and developing of those well on their way.

The suitability of a couple is often best seen in the context of community. Even how an individual person functions and contributes to others can sometimes be more readily recognized by those in the community than by the person himself. The same is true for a couple. One of the signs and results of a good marriage is that both people fit into and contribute better in the larger community. Far from becoming like a "dark hole"—like those stars whose self-oriented gravity allows no light to escape—a growing relationship brings its own kind of shining light into the lives of many.

Moreover, it is often those others in community—some older and more experienced in life, some simply close friends—who may be able to see the potential goodness, and good, of a couple, even beyond what they can see of themselves. Drawing upon a variety of insights or using some time-tested guidelines, not in isolation from life but as perceived in the context of relationships, such friends, family or community will be able to point more readily to possible suitability and rightness of fit.

Something as simple as happiness can be a measure of how a relationship is affecting a couple. Of course, any of us can be occasionally "happy" over questionable things, which we may later see as immature, weak, sinful or downright rebellious. But I am thinking here of the natural happiness that bubbles up as a result of a good relationship growing well and turning ever better. The natural interest in, and enthusiasm over, goodness is often greatly discouraged in schools, not by teachers, but by students whose goal in life is to be "cool" and unaffected by ordinary joys. However, any relationship which brings joy is wonderful, and such can be the effect of two fitting in well together.

In pointing this out, I simply desire to convey the positive and vital role of the community in the beginning, growth and deepening of marriage. Sometimes friends, family, or those with insight can see how two are, or could be, fitting in better. If such insights are conveyed with the gentleness of true wisdom, a couple can be helped to grow towards their full potential.

Those who see potential, or developing good, need to be bold enough to point it out, to encourage it, perhaps to give it direction. And there are none of us who don't need to hear of this good; all of us can benefit from the observations and feedback of those around us.

For some, such communities of relationships are almost a given in their life; but for others, there is little connection with the world outside of self. Marriage needs to be filled-out in the context of a larger community of relationships. As we learn to hear, listen, change and grow in our life conversations with others, we'll find our relationship with our spouse will be likewise deepened and enriched.

This is not to say that any community of friends, family or colleagues is perfect—far from it! We live in the imperfection of thwarted goals and crushed dreams, of old sins not forgiven, of unspoken rules strangely adhered to, of people who try to control others for an array of reasons. However, my focus in this chapter is more on a natural suitability which arises out of the creative act of God, rather than on the redemptive needs and processes of relationships. The presence and effect of sin does not do away with community, it just makes it more challenging. Moreover, we are saved into relationships, not out of them. God ministers and guides us through imperfect people; to refuse community is to refuse a normal means of grace.

I entitled this chapter "Clones & Companions" because some people search for only a mirror image of their dreams and desires in their mate; whereas what they need to find is a true companion, one with whom they complete a circle deep within both of them. We cannot predict with absolute certainty who fits best with whom. With all our advances and scientific knowledge and study of life's intricate maze, the mind cannot penetrate the mystery of the heart or of relationships. However, we can receive guidance and insights from those who live with us and know us well, and from those who have grown wise in their understanding of human relationships. Such understanding can help in forming and deepening promising relationships to the glory of God.

Biblical Illustrations and Teaching

1. In Genesis 2:18-25, there is the account of how God created Eve. Read through this account, perhaps in a few different translations. How do you and your spouse fit together? How are you partners?

2. "Do you see persons wise in their own eyes? There is more hope for fools than for them" (Proverbs 26:12, NRSV). "Fools think their own way is right, but the wise listen to advice" (Proverbs 12:15, NRSV). How good are you at receiving "advice" from your spouse? Do you have a "wise" heart which is open to hearing from someone who is different from yourself?

3. In 1 Corinthians 12:4-7, Paul mentions that there are a variety of gifts, services, and activities. How are you both better able to pursue and grow into your ministries because of your marriage? How do your ministries fit in together? How do they complement each other? What can you learn from their differences?

Little Exercises

1. They say that opposites attract. In what ways are you and your spouse "opposite," and in what ways are you similar? In what ways do you benefit each other? What are some of the long-term lessons you have, or need to, learn from the other's "differentness"?

2. List the things about your spouse that irritate you the most. Are some of them based merely on your personal

differences? Discuss these with some trusted friend (or your spouse, if your relationship is sufficiently healthy and open). Try to give thanks for at least some of these things.

3. How have people around you helped you to see the way in which you as a couple complement one another? Who can you ask about how you can further your understanding and movement towards helping the two you grow together? What things have they told you?

Chapter 4

IT COULD HAPPEN TO YOU

The Journey from the Beach to the Deep

Absalom had a beautiful sister whose name was Tamar;
and David's son Amnon fell in love with her.
2 Samuel 13:1, NRSV

Love is as strong as death.
Song of Songs 8:6

As invisible, as sure, and as powerful as the moon pulling the tides of the earth, romance has evoked an endless outpouring of story and song. In the beginning, so we read, God told the male and female to be fruitful and multiply, and fill the earth. Would that all of his commands evoked such rejoicing!

Question: What has romance to do with marriage?

"Nothing!" you say. Cynic? "Worse—experienced!"

"Everything!" another says. The icing on the cake? The little extra that pulls you through, that makes up for all the rest? The setting in which all takes place? The very foundation?

If romance dies, if you fall out of love, what will be left? I asked a friend who's close to thirty and had been going very steadily with the same girl for ten — count 'em, ten! — years, "Why don't you just get married?" His answer? "We have friends who went out for a *long* time" (did he say seven years?) "they got married, and now they're divorced—only three years later!" Why marry and spoil a good thing? Why marry, knowing that blossoms fade—as blossoms do—and desire may wither up in the dusty heat of a long day?

Does love just "happen" to you? Is it something you can conjure up—like pulling a rabbit from a magician's hat? What if you marry, and then fall in love—with somebody else! What then? Shall we forever chase after the wind, running after a will-o'-the-wisp, having one partner after another, forever dissatisfied, always open to the next breeze, another crosscurrent, to carry us somewhere else, still hoping to find ourselves in paradise?

Romance conjures up such a splattering of thoughts and memories, snapshots of moments, places, impressions and people frozen in time. A "romance" is normally thought of as a story, a tale of love, arising often out of nowhere between a man and a woman. Not so long ago, this same term was also used to refer to an adventure, like *The Romance of the High Seas*, or some such thing; it didn't necessarily have only the adventure of a particular kind of relationship in view. But how can we describe *relational* romance, and with what terms, wrung from the poverty of speech, can it be portrayed?

Romance has something to do with joy—joy particularized in a person—and it has to do with the savoring of, and getting lost in, that blissful wonder. It has to do with that one who, or the thought of whom, like the unexpected appearance of a god or goddess, evokes such spontaneous delight, whose mere presence brings joy. And imbedded in this joy, lurking near the shimmering surface of this happiness, is something too of the unknown: of danger, of excitement, of what might be, of glorious possibilities.

In romance there is something of hope; for a safe arrival at port, for the completion of the journey, for the end of the voyage. Yes, and all this regardless of the storms that may come (or so the story goes).

There is something also of faith, of an assurance that everyone—or at least all the main characters—will make it intact, that friends will be truer friends, that events both contrary and wonderful will deepen the bonds of camaraderie to unshakable allegiance. That despite all, "all's well that ends well."

It could happen to you. Ouch—look out! The sky could fall in, bits of orange and blue with fluffy white stuff stuck on it. And then what? What will you do? Abandon all for that pearl of great price? Forsaking all others, cleave only to that whispering call which fades quickly in the lush forest greens, leaving you with only the memory of the voice of an echo, the elusive glimpse of something more? Oh, if only I could fall headlong into the seas of everlasting bliss and be carried off forever! It could happen to you—don't you wish?

IN THE HAPPILY-EVER-AFTER

If only we were back in the Garden. If only Adam hadn't messed everything up. If only Eve hadn't been sidelined into that simple conversation with a snake. In the end, though, they had to leave: leave the Garden, leave Paradise, leave the idyllic setting. Nirvana was no more. Thorns and pain and struggle, all for the taste of that delicious-looking fruit, all for the desire to get a small chunk of wisdom. All because of a little lie and a quick bite.

The Garden is the perfect place for romantic fantasy. Who could resist it, or doubt it, in such a setting? Romance would blossom, and it would be great!! "Go for it!" could be the only response.

Romance on a cruise. Romance on a lost island. Romance as the moonlight shimmers off the peaceful waters. Buy your ticket, spend your thousands, climb aboard. A few weeks in the sun and who knows what might happen? You might get lucky! You might get lucky in a bar. You might get lucky in the Lotto. Who said fantasy is for children?

The world is waiting for you, so the motivational books say. Change the way you think. You can do it if you try. Create your own reality, one step at a time. Climb to the top of your dreams. You can have it all.

Problem is, there's more wrong than the Wicked Witch of the West. There's more than the ugly stepmother and horrid stepsisters to overcome. Despite Disney's constant portrayal of most creatures and most people as notably good, and only the occasional person and a few beasts as bad, real life doesn't conform to this rosy picture. There's something crucially important for children to learn about bad people and good people, but why should our view of the moral world stay at the level of a six-year-old? We could certainly all do with more encouragement, but mere enthusiasm and a better approach—the focus of so many motivational books—won't, in and of themselves, usher in our personal Utopia.

My friend Ernest thinks that the only bad people in the world are those awful hypocrites who go to church; the rest of the folks out there are pretty darn good. I admit we're a pretty mixed crowd in all those churches I've attended over the years, and it's true, as someone has well said, that it's surprising how nice those sinners are.

But maybe we've been hoodwinked; someone has pulled some thick wool over our eyes. We look at the outside of people and assume, in the absence of any notable evidence, that "all's well that looks okay." Prince Charming actually exists, and the damsel is as inwardly pure as she is outwardly beautiful. The only thing that needs changing are those rags of poverty, the rest will take care of itself, and they'll live happily ever after. We prefer to live as though nothing untoward happened in the Garden, as though we were never tainted, never shamed, never undone.

WRINKLES UNDER AN AGEING SUN

Why do we pretend that all is well? "Hope floats," you say. Sure, but hope in what? Hope about what? What are you looking for? Don't we all want to be a little happier? Can we assume that we'll find a corner of paradise in the here and now?

"Who can say, 'I have cleansed my heart, I am pure from my sin'?" (Proverbs 20:9). If we can't say that about ourselves, why do we assume that the next time will be different; that with the next person, we can start with a clean slate? Although the Western ethos is to sacrifice the state, the common good, to the rights and interests of the individual, we widen our horizons somewhat when we dream of Utopia: "Just me and my honey." With an ageing population, the American Dream is becoming either one of eventual solitude, or of retirement with that "special other."

But "there is nothing new under the sun," as the Preacher put it in Ecclesiastes (1:9). The best that one can hope for here—wealth and power, pleasures, proper religious etiquette, even righting a few wrongs—none of these come even close to ushering in the paradise of God, the New Jerusalem, the dwelling place of God come and situated fully in the midst of his people.

We cannot go back to the Garden. The future, the new heavens and earth where relationships are only right and true, all this lies before us; and for us, it has not yet come. We live in a land, a world, of shadows. "The light has come into the world, and people loved darkness rather than light because their deeds were evil" (John 3:19, NRSV). This is the preferred state of being for most of the people, most of the time. It's hard enough for Christians to be Christian—why would anyone expect better from the world? It is hard to establish Christianity in a non-Christian culture, and it is easy for that culture to slide back into darkness.

All is not well in our hearts, in our lives, in our relationships. We cannot trust that any other is pure, that any relationship can be untainted. Mixed motives abound. We may hope for the best, try as we might, but the shadows within and without are real.

Regardless, We Love

Life is uneven. People marry for every conceivable reason under the sun. Sometimes lightning may strike, the sky may fall in, poetry may flow — but maybe it won't.

Does it matter?

How can anyone know what configuration will be wonderfully marvelous, how a man and woman will best fit together?

Bill can hardly remember how many times he fell in love, but when he met Sandra, his future wife, he felt this deep, settled peace. Mary, on the other hand, met with her old boyfriend Jim just to talk about and wrap up their relationship of long ago, when suddenly, from out of nowhere, a spark of joy sprang up. From out of that peace, that joy, marriage came forth, and family.

Ted told me that, before they were married, his wife once said to him quite emphatically, "Ted, I love you, and I want to marry you!" Ted's response? "Wow, that's what I like — a woman who knows her own mind!"

Myself? I fell in love, went onto orbit, stayed out there for months, no—years! At one point, the catalyst of this ecstatic experience inquired of me, in a very gentle, wondering sort of way, "Are you sure that it's *me* you love?" And as it turned out, it wasn't! Amazing! So much for the ultimate trip. I soared off into oblivion and went nowhere. I was, as it turned out, in love with being in love. The experience was the idol.

God said, *Give me your idol.* So I did.

There you have it: a three-year pilgrimage, all to remove one idol from the temple.

But then I met my wife. And what happened? I'm not sure, but something began to happen that goes far deeper than falling in love. It is more like a homecoming, like Adam meeting Eve after they've been so long out of Paradise that they've both forgotten what it was like. They fail to even recognize each other; but there she is. I couldn't have said all this then, back there when we met, or even years later. As with most experience, my life in this respect is one of only gradual realization and understanding. I can only hope I'll live long enough to cover the basics!

There are probably as many stories as there are couples. Some stories are sad, some seem tragic, some make you wonder what on earth was happening. The best are those which manifest grace acting in the midst of darkness. Still and forever, couples are drawn together, as the moon draws steadily on the tides of the earth.

The call may come from heaven, but the responding echo can only be found as it is lived out on earth. No connection is perfect. No relationship holds within it the entirety of the Christian hope of glory. We live in the coming-but-not-yet phase of the Kingdom. Our deepest joys cannot be here, even though we *may* have some happiness, some relief, some respite.

Drawn by the warmth of love, uplifted by hope, stirred by a spark of joy; any of these, or still other things, may have been that special something which drew a certain couple together. But these reach from the past work of God in creation and in the cross; beyond the present, and—embracing all—they reach towards the future hope of "Thy kingdom come" in all its glory and fullness.

So what do we have if we cannot expect paradise? Is all lost, with respect to happiness? If romance—in whatever form—is only a foretaste of heaven, with what do we busy our hearts in the day-to-day business of married life?

Labor of Love

Please check one of the following:

- I would like to fall in love
- I would like to work at love

What shall it be: master, or victim? Fall in love, get swept away by the flood (like a quick trip I made once swimming down a fast stream, going with the flow, coasting over the rapids, stomach clenched up like a fist, until I banged enough rocks to slow down and crawl out, thankful to find shore)?

Or shall we labor towards love, standing like a rock, unmoved by floods, rooted deep, flourishing like a tree planted beside many waters, bringing forth fruit, always in green leaf, prospering in every endeavor?

Roller coasters are great fun. You get strapped in and off you go, up and down, up and around, and sometimes even upside down (for a heart-stopping, but quick, second or two). For a few minutes it's great—what a thrill! It is hard, though, to build a house on a roller coaster. The materials keep flying off, as if they had a mind of their own!

If romance is something that happens to you, who's to blame when the thrill is gone, or a new thrill arrives? One ride is over, when's the next one going to start?

Some people approach relationships like children in an amusement park. The overriding goal is *Fun! Fun! Fun!* Their only concern is to have more fun; they're consumed with the desire to have it happen to them.

Falling in love can be like that — it just happens to you. A momentary thrill, a suggestion, a glimpse; but wait—one moment more—and paradise will open up! And we expect the magic to go on forever.

Even if we're convinced that this special relationship is of God, how can we expect that a quick and effortless jump-start (those first three—or thirty—seconds, minutes, days) will necessarily mean that all will be smooth sailing till we land in port? Romance of one sort or another may have been the spark that got your relationship going, but if nothing is added after that, you'll either run aground or it'll fall apart.

What is it that smoothes our way? Can everything just "fall into place," and keep falling into place without our participation? Can our relationships just turn out right in the long run without any input from us? What is it, in the end, that brings about constancy, that builds security? Do long-term blessings just happen "willy-nilly"; do the hardships of relational calamity occur purely at random?

DEEPER THAN FUN

Sometimes when we reach the end of the esoteric, the ordinary—if we are fortunate—begins to shine forth as never before. A glimpse of heaven doesn't necessarily cause all else to be darkness; it may indeed illumine what has always been there. "The earth is the LORD'S and all that is in it" (Psalm 24:1, NRSV).

And how can we continue to delight in everyday fullness? "How can a young man keep his way pure? By living according to your word" (Psalm 119:9, NIV). But *should* Christians delight in such things? Aren't they too worldly?

Isn't it more spiritual to pretend that these earthly things aren't really important after all? In opposing those who were viewing marriage (and food) as lesser goods, the apostle Paul pointed out:

> *God has created [food and marriage] to be gratefully*
> *shared in by those who believe and know the truth. For*
> *everything created by God is good, and nothing is to be*
> *rejected, if it is received with gratitude; for it is*
> *sanctified by means of the word of God and prayer.*
>
> (1 Timothy 4:3-5)

There is nothing necessarily unholy about marriage, nor about the reasons why we would marry. We may be motivated to marry that special somebody for some reasons known to us (like being strangely moved by love, joy or peace), and very possibly for many more reasons unknown to us (see the previous chapter, and following).

On a pure feeling level, the "feeling" of romance—the excitement, enthusiasm, exhilaration—may arise for a number of reasons. The process of attraction (and repulsion!) often begins long before we understand ourselves at all. In fact, I heard one seasoned counselor state that no one really accepts himself until he is at least fifty years old — if by then!

In the beginning stages of "other" awareness, we have thoughts and images in our heads from friends, families, movies and media, parents and teachers, pastors and gurus (and, of course, our own speculations). There are hormones charging around our bodies encouraged, or discouraged, by much the same sources! We are seized with passing fantasies of paradise and momentary glimpses of ecstasy. But these are coupled with occasional encounters with strange people and the rumors and realities of marital wars—to say nothing of fallout! All of this and more makes planet Earth a strange place for propagation.

And in this context of a very strange planet, at whatever stage of growth, self-awareness, etc., you have arrived at, you may have "fallen in love." Something may have happened to you; you may be the victim of Cupid's arrow, so to speak. What then?

Ah, this is the crux of the matter. This is the issue upon which this entire chapter turns. When that magical and special "something" happens to you, how will you respond? If a piece of the sky falls on you, will you bury it (the happiness-and-marriage-are-not-of-God school of thought, not currently popular, but still possible), will you worship it (recall how I had to give up my "idol" of romance), or—and here's the tough one—will you bring it into the presence of God?

If you fall into a fast-flowing stream, no one could fault you for getting swept away. But they will fault you if indeed the water was shallow, and if by exerting yourself you could have stood up and begun to work your way back to shore.

The question of whether we *can* or *should* be willing and happy victims of romance (or whatever) depends on considerations other than the experience itself. In a culture which increasingly ranks experience above reason (at least in the relational sphere), telling "feelings" and "experience" to take a backseat is definitely not the mood of the hour.

On the other hand, we naturally prefer a good experience to last, blessedness to endure, and a journey begun to end well. We'd also just as naturally prefer to avoid trouble, stumbling over unseen obstacles, falling on thorns and experiencing only short-lived and uncertain gains. The question is how any experience—romantic or otherwise—fits into the larger picture of our lives.

BUILD TO LAST

The answer to this question—found consistently throughout Scripture—is as predictable as the sunrise, and as ordinary as daylight. What's new, if anything, is in relating what we have known, read and heard to the true center of our lives. This is always the point at which one is in danger of becoming truly Christian; not just as those who hear the word, but as those who hear it *and* act on it, in whose lives the words of life are linked to, and impressed upon, the challenges of everyday issues. The danger lies in dying to our make-belief worlds.

Consider the following litany of verses. They speak of the process of our lives as *pathways* which are clear or obscure, smooth or rough, secure or precarious. They also speak of our lives as something *built* over a period of time; like a house which eventually is blessed, or is troubled. Why is it so hard for us to believe that God is good, and that he *rewards* those who seek him? (see Hebrews 11:6). It's our own activities which make the difference! The contrast of any person's fundamental orientation, their life-direction, is highlighted in these verses:

The **path** *of the righteous is like the light of dawn,*
  that shines brighter and brighter until the full day.
The **way** *of the wicked is like darkness;*
  they do not know over what they stumble.
(Proverbs 4:18-19, emphasis mine)

God is light and in him there is no darkness at all. If we say that we have fellowship with him while we are **walking** *in darkness, we lie and do not* **do** *what is true.*
  Whoever says, "I am in the light," while hating a brother or sister, is still in the darkness. Whoever loves a brother or sister lives in the light, and in such a person there is no cause for stumbling. But whoever hates another believer is in the darkness, **walks** *in the darkness, and does not know the way to go, because the darkness has brought on blindness.*
(I John 1:5-6; 2:9-11, NRSV, emphasis mine)

Happy are those who find wisdom ... Long life is in her right hand; in her left hand are riches and honor. Her **ways** *are ways of pleasantness, and all her* **paths** *are peace. She is a tree of life to those who lay hold of her; those who hold her fast are called happy.*
  Keep sound wisdom and prudence, and they will be life for your soul ... Then you will **walk** *on your way securely and your foot will not stumble....the LORD will be your confidence and will keep your foot from being caught.*
(Proverbs 3:13, 16-18, 21-22, 23, 26, NRSV, emphasis mine)

> *Therefore everyone who hears these words of Mine, and acts upon them, may be compared to a wise man, who **built** his house upon the rock. And the rain descended, and the floods came, and the winds blew, and burst against that house; and yet it did not fall, for it had been founded upon the rock.*
>
> *And everyone who hears these words of Mine, and does not act upon them, will be like a foolish man, who **built** his house upon the sand. And the rain descended, and the floods came, and the winds blew, and burst against that house; and it fell, and great was its fall.*
> (Matthew 7:24–27, emphasis mine)

How do these lines relate to romance, to falling head over heels in love, to getting so dizzy over someone that you can't conceive of ever standing upright again? Recall that the question we are considering is this: What do you do if it happens to you, if Cupid's arrow strikes and you fall in love (or "in joy")?

RETURNING HOME

If it happens to you, go back to step one—as in Chapter One— "Marriage: It's Not about You." The same applies to all experience, from the ecstatic to the mundane. Recall Paul's explanation to Timothy again: "For everything created by God is good, and nothing is to be rejected, if it is received with gratitude; for it is sanctified by means of the word of God and prayer" (1 Timothy 4:4-5).

What would happen if everyone who flipped over that suddenly amazing person, everyone who got awash with mind-numbing feelings evoked by the mere thought or presence of that incredible "other," if all such feelings and experiences were brought into the presence of God? What would happen if, in the ongoing "living and holy sacrifice" of our lives (Romans 12:1-2), we decided to include each and every felt-experience; especially those which reach deep into our souls or which appear at the moment to consume our very being?

The righteous are those who center their lives on God, who live in the light as he is Light, who "do" the word in living by it, whose lives are turned toward the ways of trusting God and obeying him. Remember (from ChapterThree) that the "wisdom" propagated in Proverbs has as its cornerstone "the fear of the Lord"— an expression found throughout the Old Testament which incorporates virtually every form of trust and obedience.

What the above passages state is that our way in life is made smooth, secure and blessed through our own active participation; in our ever-growing and deepening relationship with God, in the constant challenge of trusting him, and in the unending need to walk obediently in his ways. In a way, things *can* fall into place, relationships *can* turn out right, but not because long-term blessings happen at random. Likewise, things can fall apart and relationships can go off the rails, but these calamities aren't just "bad luck." We are a part of what happens to us, to how things may, and do, turn out. This isn't just a New Age "create your own reality" way of reading the universe (a partial but incomplete truth). It is reflective of Scripture, like those portions of Scripture written out above.

God's intention is always to build to last. The total direction and impetus behind those texts I included above—and many, many others—is to bless us with a deep, soul-satisfying, fullness-of-life type of blessing. If you were wooed into a life-long relationship by some "echo from above," romanced in by being thawed out by love, awakened by joy, quieted by peace, that's wonderful!

Just in case you missed that last note, I'll sound it again: That's wonderful! If God isn't the author of all true and good romance, who is? (I can hear my mother cheering!) Just because the world, our flesh and the devil can soil dirt on God's creation, that doesn't mean creation is bad. Romance, like everything else, is in need of the cross. It is not pure and unadulterated, it cannot usurp the place of God, it cannot negate our obligation to love, it needs to be sanctified by means of the word of God and prayer. But it's still wonderful stuff!

However, such a glimmer of future glory is not the stopping point; it is merely the beginning. It cannot be the entire drama, nor does it contain in itself all that we need for attaining complete happiness. It is the entry into something better, deeper, fuller, more satisfying. The rest of the way is, surprisingly enough, similar to the way in which we must proceed with regard to all things:

Work out your salvation with fear and trembling;
for it is God who is at work in you,
both to will and to work for His good pleasure.
(Philippians 2:12-13)

The journey here is indeed the journey from the sandy beach to the depths of life. We can move from being a victim to being a master; from feelings that happen to choice that decides and commits and acts; from being blown away to being a free-will offering; from self-absorption to the altar; from moments of ecstasy to a journey of joy; from a vision of paradise to the paths of the righteous. The experience of romance can be the nudge towards a great adventure which, if undertaken under the guidance and direction of our Maker and Creator, can broaden and deepen our Christian life and involvement immeasurably.

Biblical Illustrations and Teaching

1. Are you convinced that such passages as Psalm 24:1 ("The earth is the LORD'S") and 1 Timothy 4:4-5 make a reasonable case for the positive place for, and existence of, romance? Why or why not?

2. What went wrong with Amnon when he "fell in love" (2 Samuel 13:1-19)? What, according to this chapter, should he have done? Could people today do that as well?

3. Which passages do you find more "convicting" with respect to your own role and responsibility for how your life and relationships evolve and progress (as written out above, in order: Proverbs 4:18-19; 1 John 1:5-6, 2:9-11; Matthew 7:24-27; Proverbs 3:13-26)? How can this affect

your ongoing commitment to establishing a good, solid and possibly marvelous marriage?

Little Exercises

1. What were the things which, as you can recall, attracted you to your spouse? Of these, are there any which need to be especially "sanctified" by the word of God and by prayer? List the teachings and passages which may help to place any of them in a broader Christian perspective.

2. Any romance can be killed by the world, the flesh, or the devil. What things in the indoctrination (or seduction) of the world, in your own life (or lives, for two of you), or from the elements of darkness have squelched that special treasuring of each other? Are there things to confess, renounce, pray over, or seek help regarding? Discuss these with a trusted spiritual friend.

3. Are you prepared to deal with unwanted romantic feelings (i.e., to or from anyone other than your spouse)? Are you sufficiently "on guard" with respect to cultivating your own relationship and ensuring that you bring all other relationships into the presence of God? Some couples tell one another of any interactions which could be tempting or dangerous. What guards do you have in place?

Chapter 5

Two to Tango

The Journey from "Perfection" to Community

Two people are better than one. . . .
A rope made out of three cords isn't easily broken.
Ecclesiastes 4:9,12, NIRV

Left hand out at waist level, hold her fingers lightly, push to go forward, pull gently to move back, move your whole body, swing your arm around to indicate change of direction. The teacher says to my wife, "Sorry, Sarah, you have to *follow* your husband in this."

These dance maneuvers—so complicated!

Our teacher in Zimbabwe, where we got our weekly exercise learning ballroom and Cha-Cha-Cha, used to joke about the couples who would come for lessons. They would make a great start, all excited about learning, and then two weeks later they'd come storming in with the divorce papers signed. Well, almost! *She* needs step-by-step instructions; *he* just wants to have fun. *He* dances with the grace of a wooden puppet; *she* puts heart and soul into every move.

In our case, she (being my wife) just wants to get out there and *do* it, and he (poor soul) can't for the life of him remember what the teacher said last week. And so I'd ask my usual questions: How was I supposed to stand? How am I supposed to hold my hand? Which foot goes forward first? When do I start? Which dance is this, anyway?

Sure, "it takes two to tango," but it takes a lot more than just being there to get it!

Give and take, step at a time. My wife responds to music from her innermost being. My total physical response to music is usually limited to adjusting the volume. What's wrong with me? I have a good pedigree; my mother would just float to music! On the other hand, my father—as he would often say—"had two left feet," and "couldn't hold a tune in a bucket."

"It's so easy to be led by the *teacher*," my wife would exclaim, looking at me with that "so what's wrong with *you*?" expression.

It's one thing to file away this general thought: *People learn differently.* It's quite another to be stuck with someone who is so unspeakably frustrating as they ruin your progress (almost deliberately, it appears!) with their innate and seemingly inane inabilities.

On the other hand, if it's "My way, or the highway!", then the world will become filled with isolated strangers, unable to communicate, interact or understand each other.

DIFFERENCES, DIFFERENCES, DIFFERENCES

People learn differently: some by doing, some by step-by-step instructions, some by seeing it done.

But people also *see* differently. They focus on different things, they value differently, compute differently, and express themselves differently.

How does this play itself out in everyday life?

When I took my six-year-old daughter to her new school, I barely noticed the kids running around as I scanned the buildings looking for the right doors. Suddenly, out of the blue, my daughter asked me, "Did you see how high those boots were?" What? Where? I quickly looked at the nearest first grade kids, but they were wearing running shoes. "No! Over *there*," I was told. Oh, those *eighth* grade girls who walked by two minutes ago — *their* boots. Funny I didn't notice that!

Like mother, like daughter. The females of my family are finely attuned to clothing, styles, hair, who is talking to whom, manner of expression, and so on. All very relational and external sort of stuff.

Some people enjoy fiddling around in the shop. Some like poking about and forever fine-tuning their car. Some prefer piecing together elaborate puzzles. I live a distinct amount of time in my head, fiddling with and fine-tuning certain kinds of ideas, and seeing how they fit together. My wife, wonderful practical creature that she is, is usually far more interested in the "so what?" aspect of, well, virtually anything. She's also a natural at communicating for *impact*, whereas I am more naturally attuned to the *content* of what's being said.

Communication: What a constant challenge! Back in seminary, we had to "stand and deliver" in preaching class. How well I remember a friend's feedback after my very first sermon, which he tactfully held back until we were on our way home together. Although he had sat in the second row of a three-row classroom, he followed his opening (and kindly-intended) comment, "That was a pretty good sermon," with the remark, "although, to be honest, I could hardly *hear* most of it."

Wow. All those pearls of wisdom turned to vapor before even getting ten feet away from this storehouse of hard-won information!

With equal content but more volume, I delivered my first sermon for a "live" audience at a downtown mission. My someday-to-be-wife, focused as usual on clear and impactful communication, commented afterwards, "It'd be good if you *looked* at the audience sometimes." What?! Look at the audience? Connect with the congregation? But then I'd lose my train of thought! I am told this is a typical weakness of an idea-oriented person.

Differences. Typical strengths, typical weaknesss. The stronger the strength, the weaker the weakness.

And where are we going with all this?

Rule: When I am strong, then I am weak; but when I am weak, then I am strong.

Moreover, the same holds for relationships.

Conquer through Weakness

What good is content if you can't communicate? All those brilliant thoughts, all that hard-won know-how, all locked away. On the other hand, what good is eloquence if you have nothing to say? Some people can talk for hours—about nothing!

What good is it being practical if you don't know which course of action is better? What's the use in being wildly enthusiastic, if you can't discern where best to put all that energy?

The speaker needs to find something to say. The thinker needs to learn how to communicate. The active and energetic need to get clear on what they should be doing.

"Two *are* better than one" (Ecclesiastes 4:9, emphasis mine). The self-reliant, all-powerful, completely competent individual is an utter myth. We need others to fill in our deficiencies, to make up for what we lack, to be strong where we are weak.

If all that I can see is all that I can see, I am limited to my own horizons, I am imprisoned by my own resources. Moreover, I am deficient in my strength; I can do nothing other than what I can do. These tautologies—as in (supposedly) self-evident truths—are somewhat humbling! Give and take, one step at a time. God in his wisdom has not left us marooned, alone and solitary, on some distant island, left entirely to the accumulated resources of one person.

Just to make the point, I'll put it into one very long sentence (so, buckle up!). No one person can be all things, do all things, see all things, sense all things, intuit all things; dream of hidden potential, make good use of what's been given; inspire, exhort, give oversight, sort out detail, care for the hurting, go where no one has gone before, keep the home fires burning, fathom the enduring good of the past, perceive the way for the future, be utterly present in the present, listen well, instruct with a story, lighten the mundane with a joke, stay with the needy, endure with the suffering, make lunch for the kids, grow deep in solitude, lead the ladies' Bible study, bring justice to the oppressed, evangelize the lost, help Bob with his tractor, and in all things be utterly oriented to God, who is over all.

Enter the Church.

When Paul was responding to the issue of relationships in the Church, the new society of God on which the Spirit had been poured out, he described it in terms of a body with many parts, or members. He wrote, "There are many members, but one body. And the eye cannot say to the hand, 'I have no need of you'; or again the head to the feet, 'I have no need of you'" (1 Corinthians 12:20-21). If all the items mentioned above are any indication, there is no way that any one of us can say "I have no need of you" to the Body of Christ.

There's simply no way that any one person can love God and neighbor in a comprehensive and thorough way, all alone. The task is just too great!

Including *That* One!?

If we cannot say to the Body of Christ—or even to any one member of it—"I have no need of you," how is it that so many of us are tempted to say "I have no need of you" to our spouse? How can we pretend to be strong, independent, self-sufficient, unquestionably competent, fearless, impressive, altogether resourceful, and completely without need for help of *any* kind (be it input, encouragement, wisdom, perspective, information, alternative interpretations, obtainable goals, workable means, vision, compassion, prayer. . .and on the list goes)?

Was it not God who said, "It is not good for the man to be alone" (Genesis 2:18), and then created the first community, consisting of a man and a woman, a husband and a wife? This togetherness is as much a part of the created order as the birds of the air and the fish in the sea. That first man was *deficient* in and of himself. He needed another, and not simply a creature—like all those who were paraded before him for naming (see Genesis 2:19)—nor an angel divine. He needed one who, like himself, was something of both: a creature, and yet divine. And in time, God fashioned one who corresponded to the needy one.

Perhaps in saying these things I am speaking more to men than to women. In the original story, it was the man who was needy; and even later, God told the woman she would still desire her husband—despite the pain involved (Genesis 3:16). It seems to me that men have a basic need of women, whereas women don't "need" men, at least in quite the same way. Moreover, in a male-female relationship, men seem more task-oriented, much like Adam tilling the ground (this I have heard, as well as seen); whereas women seem more preoccupied, not with a task *per se*, but with the man himself, with being in relationship, and with "helping" that particular man.

Perhaps this is why females seem to be more relational and communicative; part of their primary role with respect to those needy males is to "connect." This does not mean that males aren't relational or communicative (they can be greatly), but often they can even turn these things into a task, instead of a process whereby one connects with another.

To whatever extent these thoughts are valid (for culture and the curse of sin always affect what is—or may have been—"natural"), this means that in any marriage relationship there is a basic underlying premise. The man, in effect, looks to the woman in this regard, "I *need* you (to be a help for me)," and the woman regards the man correspondingly, "I really 'need' (or, greatly yearn) to be a help for you." Of course, nobody actually *says* these things, but there they are: a basic subtext, an unspoken mind-set, informing the very foundation of the entire relationship.

And the strength of that relationship is dependant upon how weak, so to speak, the man and woman are willing to be with respect to each other; how readily they are willing to admit or to act out their need to ask for, give and receive help.

A Soft Rain

In some countries, the change from the dry season to the rainy season is very important. This was certainly the case in Zimbabwe, where we lived for five years during "the worst drought in living memory"—as every other newspaper article reminded us!

If the first rains that come are "hard" rains, the water just rolls off the surface of the ground and it does little good. The ground itself is too hard and nothing can penetrate. What is needed, before any large quantity of rain falls, are the "soft" rains. These lighter rains soften up the earth and make it possible for the later rains to really soak in.

What is it that is needed for the "muchness" of marriage—for the coming together on innumerable levels—to have its effect?

What is needed are two hearts which have been softened, opened, made willing and able (or at least learning) to take in, to receive, to grow.

In the complexity of human relationship, endeavor and everyday living, the many ways any particular couple fit together are probably best perceived by a sharp-eyed observer who knows both of them very well and has seen them close at hand over the course of many years and through a variety of situations.

However, it is not necessary for the mystery of marriage to be fully known, understood, analyzed and described in order for it to happen. What is necessary is for the two involved to be always and ever open to growing into the depth and reality of marriage.

This means that I must always be open to my spouse, that I must work against closing myself off. The mind-sets of "I don't need you" or "I refuse to be a help to you" are death to the relationship. When the "I" is strong and at the center of focus, the "us" is weak and at the outside edge. When I am "strong"—utterly independent, self-sufficient, set apart from my spouse, absorbed in the strength of my own strength, in the brilliance of my own glory—then our relationship becomes weak. But when I am "weak"—willing to be humble, open, vulnerable, honest, deficient, direct and truthful with my spouse—then the relationship which exists between us becomes strong.

How hard it is to admit to having need. Who wants to admit to not having some ability or knowledge, to not being self-sufficient at least in some areas?! It's even worse not being able to understand exactly what it is that you don't understand. It's hard to feel "dumb," to grow aware of some mysterious lack. In fact, it can be downright painful!

Some people are so aware of their own brilliance, they're completely unable to see their shortcomings and deficiencies. Nor can they see how amazingly incredible others are—

especially at things that they themselves don't usually even notice.

This focus on our inborn needs is not to say that the woman should become a mere instrument to fulfill the man's projects or desires; such a state is distinctly unChristian and dehumanizing, although it is altogether too frequently a reality. Nor should the man become a mere project for the woman to form (or more likely *re*-form) into an image of her own design; such a state is also distinctly unChristian and dehumanizing, although it is occasionally a reality.

Part of becoming ever more Christian, and ever less "worldly," is departing from and overcoming temptations towards such forms of ungodliness. Respect for the other person as an integral part of God's creation, and cherishing the other for who they are in themselves, is essential to a proper growing and fitting in together over time. This realization, and acceptance, of our need of others, and of our spouse, is the "soft rain" which opens us up to learning. But this is simply to point out part of the beginning of the journey.

Hard Rains - Hard Ground

How do we respond to our spouse? Too often, we rain hard on those nearest and dearest. Their ground may be hard and in need of input, but instead of softening it up, we react in harshness. We rain criticism instead of compassion.

We all need to be told, in the context of community, in the midst of real relationships, what we are good at, and where our deficiencies lie. Otherwise we are left guessing, permanently unsure of what we can and can't do well, where we should put our best efforts, and what endeavors we should better leave to those more naturally, or supernaturally, gifted. What better context to learn this than marriage, and from someone who is—often enough—our chief defender and advocate, believing in us more than we do ourselves?

In the real world, are people so kindly, insightful and helpful? Sometimes yes, but sometimes no. But it is helpful to make a distinction between where we ourselves are at and where we would like to be. Each one is deficient in terms of creation; no one person can be and do all things. But we are doubly deficient in terms of our need for redemption. Sin has darkened and twisted our perceptions of ourselves and others, stunted our personal growth, and entangled our interpersonal and communal lives in an endless maze of unreal roles and oppressive expectations.

In dealing with some difficult Christians, Paul appealed to them "by the meekness and gentleness of Christ" (2 Corinthians 10:1). He was seeking to show the same attitude as Christ: "I who am meek when face to face with you" (v. 1), even though these people were opposing him. Many would find this quality of character to be almost impossible when speaking with a spouse who seems—and maybe is!—dead set in opposition. It's sometimes easier to blast the other, to speak in the terse tones of sheer frustration, about what *we* think is so totally obviously wrong.

There is a journey involved in learning how to give. The rightness of our insights and perspectives doesn't depend upon our kindness and skill in relating them. Understanding our spouse's vulnerability, uncertainties, and difficulty in admitting need may help to soften the tone of our critique, but at some point before perfection arrives (for either spouse), what needs to be said should somehow be said—and hopefully in ways the other can understand.

There is also a journey involved in learning how to receive. How hard it is to be ignored! To have something of worth to say, something of value to contribute, an insight that penetrates dark clouds of gloomy confusion, hope bubbling up from an eternal fountain of faith, creative juices flowing with endless possibilities, but all to no end; all trodden underfoot, overlooked, disregarded or brushed aside like some bothersome fly. To be consigned to a solitary role, like "bringing home the bacon," or "merely" childbearing; this is to fall so far short of the glory of God.

Like doing the tango or a waltz all alone, how contradictory it is to be in a relationship, while at the same time not being willing—or able—to play a part in that relationship. There needs to be that give-and-take, a willingness to go a step at a time, to learn, to advance, to move from the known into the unknown, to lead, to follow.

CLOSED MIND, OPEN HEART

In writing this I am very conscious that I am speaking as a male and a husband. When my wife, who completed a degree in music, expressed interest in learning the violin, I couldn't relate to how it thrilled her soul, but I encouraged her to start lessons. After a necessary break—due to her bearing our daughter—I encouraged her to take it up again. How shocked I was to hear her say that, actually, there was something she really wanted to do, that she had *always* wanted to do, but she was afraid to say so.

What on earth could she like more than playing violin, which she had spoken of and raved about for years? Her hesitation arose from her knowledge of me; for she had always *really* wanted to learn dance—since she was a little girl—but that required a partner! I immediately determined not to be one of those reluctant husbands (note: this required a *deliberate* decision!), and we checked out and found a great studio and, I might add, a very patient teacher!

I'd love to do a poll of how many wives read the above story and say to their husbands, "Look, *he* learned — why can't *you*?!" There seem to be far more women than men who like to respond to music with movement, with dance and (dare I say it) with a *partner!*

There also seem to be far more women who want to make a relationship work, who are willing to check out and understand the mysteries of what makes relationships work well. But it does take two to tango. You cannot have a strong relationship if you are not willing to admit to weakness. You cannot make progress towards completion unless you're willing to admit to being deficient. You cannot have two together unless you're willing to become more than just one. You have to be willing to soften up on the hard rain. You have to be willing to soften up your own hard ground. And you have to be willing to receive from another.

Consider how Proverbs conveys this basic and fundamental need for receiving from others in our relationships (all from NRSV):

The ear that heeds wholesome admonition
 will lodge among the wise (15:31).
Fools think their own way is right,
 but the wise listen to advice (12:15).

Whoever heeds instruction is on the path to life,
but one who rejects a rebuke goes astray (10:17).
Those who ignore instruction despise themselves,
but those who heed admonition gain understanding
(15:32).
Whoever loves discipline loves knowledge,
but those who hate to be rebuked are stupid (12:1).
Pleasant words are like a honeycomb,
sweetness to the soul and health to the body (16:24).
With patience a ruler may be persuaded,
and a soft tongue can break bones (25:15).
A soft answer turns away wrath,
but a harsh word stirs up anger (15:1).
A gentle tongue is a tree of life,
but perverseness in it breaks the spirit (15:4).
Why should fools have a price in hand to buy wisdom,
when they have no mind to learn? (17:16).
A fool takes no pleasure in understanding,
but only in expressing personal opinion (18:2).
Listen to advice and accept instruction,
that you may gain wisdom for the future (19:20).

Anyone can have a closed mind, but we can choose to open our hearts. Regardless of how much of our ground is hard, or how we just habitually and instinctively rain real hard on others, there is always the upward call to a better way: it is ours for the taking. "For the wise the path of life leads upward, in order to avoid Sheol [the place of death] below" (15:24, NRSV).

SNIP AND TUCK, AND SNIP, AND TUCK, AND ...

We look for perfection in any potential spouse. And as the wedding day comes closer, as we move closer to marrying into a new circle of family and friends, the mixed condition of our "perfect" spouse may become ever more clear. What appears glorious at a distance may (as is often the case) looks questionable upon closer inspection. "Never look a gift horse in the mouth"—you may just discover its real age! Never expect that spouse sent from heaven to look—or act—like an angel forever. It won't happen! The vast amount of work put into making the wedding day "just right" reveals just how "imperfect" ordinary days are, and how hard it is to *look* perfect, even for such a short period of time.

Israel's collected wisdom from centuries of sages ends with an alphabetically arranged poem, the "ABC's" of the *perfect* wife (Proverbs 31:10–31; of course, the ABC's follow the Hebrew alphabet). This poem opens with the question, "An excellent wife, who can find?" (v. 10), and near its end, children and husband rise up to praise such a woman: "Many daughters have done nobly, but you excel them all" (v. 29). The next line explains why: "Charm is deceitful and beauty is vain, but a woman who fears the LORD, she shall be praised" (v. 30).

The implications of this woman "fearing God"—as far as the husband is concerned—are mentioned in the second and third verses of this poem:

> *The heart of her husband trusts in her, and he will have*
>   *no lack of gain.*
> *She does him good and not harm, all the days of her life*
>   (vv. 11–12 NRSV).

The rest of this poem itemizes numerous ways in which this wonderful woman "does him good" throughout the entirety of her life.

So what does it mean to ask a young man, "Where could you find such a *perfect* woman?", and then turn around and point to one of the elderly women sitting nearby and answer, "She's right there — your *mother*!"? What this does is that it highlights the time span contained in this poem. It changes the common perception that the young man will—or should—look for all such accomplishments and qualities in a young, prospective, yet-to-be wife. Rather, the young man needs to realize that perfection comes only over time, in the long run.

Likewise, a young woman may not only strive to have these qualities, she may also take some relief in the fact that these things come to fruition over a lifetime of living. Godly character takes time to develop. Many of the activities mentioned throughout this poem could not possibly be done in each and every twenty-four-hour time period; they are the culmination of effort over many months, if not years! Most of the things mentioned are customary or occasional actions, like buying a field and planting a vineyard (as in v. 16 — not something you'd do every morning!). These were normal activities of a diligent and "smart" wife in ancient Israel, the kind of activities which revealed, over time, praise-worthy character.

On one level, we are drawn to someone who is a "perfect match." Yet on a deeper level, we need to be drawn to someone with whom we can grow. The two of you can learn together, and you can even learn *how* to learn, together. This requires humility, but it's the kind of humility which precedes a good game. You submit to the rules and wholeheartedly work to overcome all obstacles which keep you from progressing towards the goal. You win when you *both* win. Don't quit the dance just because your partner is not perfect yet! Winning requires all participants to take the game seriously, and to keep playing.

Loving, respecting and cherishing the other may have a good and natural start in the initial stages of a positive relationship, but these things need to be deliberately and actively pursued and strengthened throughout the entire course of marriage.

A man is not to serve his own goals and projects, but God. Likewise, a woman needs to deliberately place God in centre of her relationships, especially with her husband.

Conversely, a woman is not to serve her own goals and projects, but God. Likewise, a man needs to deliberately place God in centre of his relationships, especially with his wife.

The woman needs to be loved for who she is in herself, and appreciated for her invaluable support and involvement. The man needs to be respected for who he is, for what he does, for his dreams, etc. The command for the woman to respect her husband, and for the husband to love his wife, is clear in Ephesians 5:33. Many marriages are troubled, some beyond hope, because these two "game rules" are not adhered to.

Marriage is a holy estate—as the marriage ceremony puts it—and not to be entered into lightly. Marriage is also a commitment to a lifelong process, and perfection doesn't come easily. Like the concert pianist whose ten-hours-a-day practice routine makes playing look easy, like the martial artist who can do amazing feats only after decades of rigorous practice, so the full glory of marriage comes with time; time and patience and learning how to play well in this very serious and wonderfully wonderful game of holy matrimony.

When I am weak, we are strong.

In the journey of marriage, each one needs to become a full and active participant, both giving and receiving. Each needs to move from the "perfection" of one (whichever one that may be!) to the community of both.

Let us together enter fully into the weakness of being human, into the limitation of being "one," so that we may enter into the divine glory of working together towards true marriage.

Biblical Illustrations and Teaching

1. In the Body of Christ it's okay to be "incomplete." In 1 Corinthians 12, Paul speaks about various abilities, ministries, positions (vv. 4-5), and some wrong attitudes about such differences (vv. 12-26). Who do you have, or display, such attitudes toward ("I don't need them," or, "They're not really one of us")? How could you change this?

2. In James 4:6-10 and 5:16, there is a mix of pride and humility, sin and confession. Beyond natural or spiritual

incompleteness, it's okay to be broken and in need of redeeming grace. What things block a more effective working together in your marriage?

3. "Do you see a man wise in his own eyes? There is more hope for a fool than there is for him" (Proverbs 26:12). Reflect on the proverbs listed in the "Hard Rains - Hard Ground" section. How do you measure up in the context of your relationship? [Note that 'the wise' and 'the fool' can be ideals (positive or negative), an orientation, or a momentary lapse.]

Little Exercises

1. Make a short list of some of the most "useless" people you know. Begin to give thanks for these folks. Ask God to enable you to see the different gifts and abilities they have. Find out why other people appreciate them.

2. What are some of your strengths? What are your weaknesses? What about your spouse? Try having each of you make a short list of these, and then exchange them. Starting with the stronger strengths, and the lesser weaknesses, how can you develop your strengths together, and counteract your weaknesses?

3. Try to grow aware of how you already offset your spouse's weaknesses and/or deficiencies, and how your spouse counteracts your own. Express open appreciation of these, as a basis for developing an even greater openness for growing together.

Chapter 6

Somebody Else's Paradise

The Journey from the Physical to the Personal

Godliness with contentment is great gain.
1 Timothy 6:6, NIV

Question: Do you believe it?

STRIPPED, BEATEN, AND HALF-DEAD

Albert Einstein supposedly remarked that heaven consists of one giant library, where one could take out books with no time limit. When I was young, the idea of eternal life actually sounded screamingly dull, like the long, quiet Sunday afternoons I passed as a child; unable to do certain outdoor sports because it was "the Lord's day," and unable to make much noise because mom and dad were catching up on some much-needed sleep.

Today's society has a much quicker view of "the good life," consisting mainly of brief moments of unparalleled ecstasy. At least this is the red flag waved in the eyes of the young and the energetic.

The less energetic—either by age, natural disposition, or circumstance—may go for slower, or more peaceful, pleasures. Pride of place, attaining long-earned accomplishments, or finally securing a high position — these things are given a quiet nod of approval. But for general interest in the fast-paced dominant culture, all is subservient to the prevailing thirst of our time: The quest for pleasure.

As long as we are free to pursue whatever brings us happiness, as long as the happy state of others is enhanced, the world can be seen as through rose-tinted glasses. Popularity is ensured to those artists, singers, writers, leaders and politicians who explicitly or by silence bless this our obsession; my quest for what makes me feel good. As long as I can do what I please, when I want, with whomever, then you can do and say what you want. Just leave me alone.

This is paradise without God, without any of those bothersome Divine Beings who constantly design ways and plot to constrain the headlong lemming-like rush of these poor creatures, whose only wish is to die content in the ocean of sweet happiness. We only want gods—and, of course, goddesses!—who are free and able to do what we can only dream of doing, so we can join in vicariously, so we can sin through their sinning.

This is the world of Hollywood and multimedia, where the heroes and heroines are those who have a little gold mixed in with their otherwise very common clay. Good looks, talent of sorts, and a wayward life ensure a quick route to immortality, at least for a time. The hard-won advancements of science are picked up and pressed into the propagation of an easier life. Hard-fought political advancements around the globe are heralded for securing our own sense of security, wherein we can continue to pursue what ordinary pleasures are available to us.

This spells disaster for marriage.

We have more sex and less intimacy. Shame consists in falling out of social favor. Contentment is for those who have nothing. The drive to make nakedness and nudity commonplace wars against the soul, individually and collectively. This is Paradise on the near side of Hell, on the picnic grounds just outside of Hell's tinsel gates. The gates of Hell may not prevail against the Church, but they're sure doing a good job of it in the world.

How close would we have to get to our most intimate friend or spouse to see what we see of models and actors, whose faces and body parts are displayed so much larger than life on the screens and billboards across the landscape? This is intimacy at a distance, two-dimensional familiarity, poses paper-thin and timeless, in-your-face and unasked for, masquerading a given nearness, providing a dreamy distraction from the complexity of life, from the curse and blessing of society's maze-like structure of how real relationships happen—or not!

Everybody smiles for the camera. We see what we want to see. Buried are the tensions, games, doubts, quarrels, wounds, deprivations, gossip and egos. All's well that looks well.

In such an environment, can we pretend to be so pure? Can we pretend to come to the physical union integral to marriage as though we were innocent babes? Our minds and perspectives, our hopes and dreams of knowing and being known, our trust and expectations—these have all been tainted, skewed, distorted, maligned, damaged, and made grossly deficient. Like the man who traveled down from Jerusalem to Jericho in Jesus' parable of the Good Samaritan, we have fallen into the hands of robbers and been left stripped, beaten, and half-dead.

So Near, So Distant

The people on the elevator stare woodenly at the numbers blinking overhead. Soon their various floor numbers will flash, and off they go. So close, yet saying nothing. Strangers unwilling to even stare at the outsides of those who could stare back. Obviously such staring is rude, as we quickly tell the children.

Yet we stare at strangers all the time. Looking is easier than talking. We watch and wonder, *What makes him tick? Where is she going in such a hurry? What is the nature of their relationship? Is he kind? Is she friendly? Do they have it in for me?*

Talking takes time. Babbling takes up time, but it doesn't advance relationship. Talking, on the other hand, real conversing back and forth, that takes time and energy. People are deep, lives and experience accumulate, and getting to know another takes forever.

So what does all of that have to do with sex? Ouch! Did I suggest something out of order; like relating knowing someone sexually to actually *knowing* them? Odd connection, that!

To the horny, the inexperienced, the shy and quiet, the loud and boisterous, the lonely and the well-connected, the world shouts a very noisy monotone: Sex offers that singular, brief moment of unparalleled ecstasy you've always been looking for.

If I die without having had sex, reasoned the young soldier, *I won't have really lived*. Fortunately for him, the young nurse agrees to his advances, and the movie camera modestly loses focus as the band plays a stirring tune.

Really, Hollywood could take virtually any moment in life, from the cradle to the grave, and make it the moment of decisive ecstasy. Instead of dramatizing the screams of the mother in childbirth (giving young girls nightmares), they could slowly dwell upon "the moment after," with the young, squirming babe making its first squeaks, and waving about its pudgy little fingers and toes. Family and friends could gather near, oohing and awing, laughing and telling jokes. A moment of celebration, the momentary pain forgotten, paling into insignificance in the face of a miracle newly-born.

This one baby could be the culmination of years of effort, of searching for the "right mate," of losing one or two children in childbirth, of despairing of ever having the joy of raising your own children. Or, the focus could be on the beginning, on the years of growth and development and family and social functioning all wrapped up in the miracle of this little baby.

To be honest, I'm telling somebody else's story. Neither my family nor my society has predisposed me to see babies in this way. How many are rootless and groundless, ahistorical and shortsighted, living in the here and now, with no future and no past? How on earth is one to gain any perspective on life's normal processes if your time horizon is five years, eighteen months, or less? When I was thirteen, seventeen was old, and I never really expected to live beyond twenty. There were no elders in that world, just some people who got old, who watched life speed by from the sidelines.

Youth is eternal, beauty is all.

Okay, youth is a moment, and beauty is a matter of perspective; but this isn't going to sell much in the way of associative advertising!

Youth is a moment in a life that stretches from the cradle to the grave. Youth doesn't have to be a dead end, nor can it be a "thing-in-itself." The context for youth is life, all of life: from the baby to the toddler, to the young kid at school, to the growing youth, to the young woman and young man moving out into the widening world of social and vocational relationships, to getting established and experienced, to assuming greater responsibilities, to giving the strength and creativity of one's best years to people and projects and endeavors, to maturing and gaining perspectives on life and relationships, to the settled and quieter accumulation of clear wisdom and simple enjoyments. Youth is a moment in a life that can stretch from the cradle to the grave. There is no need to rob it of its meaning.

The meaning of youth is rooted in the past and stretches out beyond the present towards the future.

As with youth, so with—not beauty—but sex.

Sex is not a moment. Sex is—as with everything human—both history and future, common and sacred, animal (or creaturely) and spiritual. Moreover, sexual union creates, secures and affirms a special sort of relational bond, a bond between the participants; it is a deep and unique sort of intimacy, one whose impact resounds into the innermost recesses of the human psyche.

Contrary to popular belief, you *can* have intimacy without sex (shocking, but true!). An unnecessary corollary is that you can have sex without intimacy (just as many fear!). The first is "normal" in varying degrees in most healthy, long-term relationships of virtually any sort. The second is a sad deficiency; it is also a lie.

Consuming Fire

There is nothing casual about meeting God, that consuming fire of warmth and fidelity. If you were thinking about entering the Holy of Holies in Israel's ancient temple—an area reserved for an annual visit by select priests—you'd have to get someone to tie a rope around your ankle, just in case you got struck dead and they had to drag you out.

There is also nothing casual about approaching the innermost recesses of ourselves or of another, in real relationship or by implication. There is no such thing as "safe sex."

Intimacy is hazardous to all concerned.

Every culture has its acquaintance distance, its friendship distance, and its intimate distance. When we enter someone else's intimate distance, or someone enters your intimate—or personal—space, there's an immediate response: either repulsion or attraction. This emotional response is completely natural, almost instinctive—unless, of course, you're emotionally dead. Emotional starvation often precedes emotional death, and nothing hastens that death like surrogate forms and images masquerading as intimacy.

Sex without intimacy is foisted upon us at every turn: media, advertisements, TV, book covers, billboards, wherever. In this way, we have "more sex," but less intimacy.

Not only is it more, it is more meaningless, a wasteland which grows like a cancer in the soul, a chasm ever-deepening into an abyss. This is the way of sexuality without source and foundation, without eternal perspective, with only the here-and-now of momentary experience in view, a drive-through mind-set of mechanical exchanges, physical approximation mingled with personal alienation; but what do you expect?

Staring at strangers is rude; it dehumanizes them. Staring at naked strangers is doubly rude; it denudes, destroys, and dehumanizes the soul of the beholder. It's rude whether they've been painted onto the side of a wall, or they're getting steamed up on a giant screen in the cinema. We live in a rude age, an age that corrupts, an age that taints, an age that turns normal developmental questions and normal wonderings on their heads and spins them off in twenty directions. Our technology blesses us with healthier bodies and longer lives, but it curses us with deformed souls and lifeless relationships, and only we are to blame.

In this world, confusion is normal. At least, it should come as no surprise; for what the world offers is so often far more than anything it can deliver. Lies, deceptions, and half-truths can never deliver. We are not closer for all the illusion of closeness. Photographs and films cannot affect relational intimacy no matter what they show, despite the fact they may create the feeling—or the illusion—of intimacy.

On the other hand, sexual intimacy with strangers—even at a distance—rots the soul:

For a prostitute's fee is only a loaf of bread,
*   but [the adulteress] stalks a man's very life.*
Can fire be carried in the bosom
*   without burning one's clothes?*
He who commits adultery has no sense;
*   he who does it destroys himself.*
(Proverbs 6:26, 27, 32, NRSV)

Although this text was originally aimed towards male listeners, I have no doubt that the same could be said for females. Adultery destroys the soul. And not just physical adultery, but likewise sexual intimacy at-a-distance; for "everyone who looks at a woman with lust has already committed adultery with her in his heart" (Matthew 5:28, NRSV). This is the way of this generation, "having eyes full of adultery … [and] a heart trained in greed" (2 Peter 2:14); and in the end, any "greed" is a form of idolatry (see Colossians 3:5).

Confusion arises in our minds, for who is willing to destroy the golden idol? Pleasure is by its very nature transient; it lasts for a moment. How can you "build to last" on shifting sand? It doesn't make sense. No wonder confusion sets in — we just don't make sense. Physical intimacy without a personal relationship makes us no better than a dog on the street; only the darkness in the soul deepens.

Confusion arises in our hearts. We set our tastes for eternity, and end up spitting dust. There is no stability in that which is so elusive. We need something greater to make sense of something lesser. Every society, every people, every culture errs in some way; ours makes a special case for "seek your own pleasure without restraint and without restriction." This focus on the transient mocks our quest for the eternal, our yearning for solid joys and lasting pleasures without ceasing.

Only the one who is rooted in the eternal, in the sacred, in the spiritual, can well and truly savor the momentary, the common, the creaturely. For "the world is passing away, and also its lusts; but the one who does the will of God abides forever" (1 John 2:17). And as another apostle said to those who saw the physical union of marriage as unspiritual, "Everything created by God is good, and nothing is to be rejected, provided it is received with thanksgiving; for it is sanctified by God's word and by prayer" (1 Timothy 4:4-5, NRSV).

The world idolizes small particles, little aspects of life, tearing them from their right relation to God and eternity and the sacred, and in so doing empties them of joy. God's real intent is not to render us a joyless existence; rather, Scripture exhorts us to believe that he alone is the guarantor, the author and perfecter, of all true joy.

Narrow Pathway, Large World

What evokes wonder?
And what reveals a wasteland?

Three things are too wonderful for me;
 four I do not understand:
 the way of an eagle in the sky,
 the way of a snake on a rock,
 the way of a ship on the high seas,
 and the way of a man with a girl.
This is the way of an adulteress:
 she eats, and wipes her mouth,
 and says, "I have done no wrong."
 (Proverbs 30:18-20, NRSV)

"The way of a man with a girl" evokes wonder; "the way of an adulteress" reveals a wasteland.

The glory of oneness. It is there, beckoning.
This is the way of God:
 to join the transience of momentary experience to
  both the past and the future;
 to join the common to the sacred;
 to join the creaturely to the spiritual;
 to sanctify that special sort of relational bond
  which sexual union creates, secures and
   affirms;
 to ensure that this deep and unique sort of
   intimacy,
   whose impact resounds into the innermost
    recesses of the human psyche,

has a lifetime to allow its roots to travel
deeper than any other can;
for its fruit flourishes ever more fully with each
passing season,
a process for which a lifetime is far too short.

This is only a part of the glory of oneness.

ONE YES, A THOUSAND NO'S

The dew is on the grass, dripping from the petals, clinging to the garden webs; beauty beckons, joy awaits, the war is on.

"What war?" you ask. The war against all that would distract either one of you from continuing long-term with the other, from growing ever deeper into the unique kind of wonderfulness that can only be found in marriage. We are drawn into a relationship, sometimes for the ecstasy and joy of just being with that other, sometimes for the joy and ecstasy of the *other* person in being with us. But what begins well—with all the right intentions in the world—does not exist in a vacuum.

Is she cute? So is one of her friends. Is he strong? So are some of his buddies. Is that so surprising? After all, "Birds of a feather flock together."

Is she fun-loving and spontaneous, organized to a "t," great at meeting new people, brilliant at getting things done? So are some of her friends. Is he quiet and thoughtful, predictable and dependable, full of strange and different ideas? So are some of the handful of those he makes a point of conversing with regularly.

The above paragraph describes a bit of what Sarah and I are like (except for the organized part), but what of it? Is she the only one in the world with a number of these qualities? Amazingly, no. Is he the only one like this? No again.

Opposites attract; but there's more than one opposite out there.

Moreover, birds of a feather *do* flock together. It's a very good chance that, naturally speaking, a number of his or her closer friends are close opposites.

There are no clones, of course. Even twins differ. And the more a twosome journey together along the road to becoming one, the more unique that other one is found to be, as a person and not as a conglomeration of attractive characteristics.

It is natural to be attracted to the same kind of person. There are, in all likelihood, a number of potential "runner-ups," a short string of "close but no cigar" contestants (either real or imagined) somewhere out there. And surprisingly enough, they don't all die the day we walk down the aisle and say "I do" to that very special one.

All of this is to say that the commitment to that one other person—the saying of "I do" and "I will" at all the right moments—does not end on the wedding day. It began when you followed up on that initial glance, when you left an opening for that other to respond, and it does not end "until death do you part."

So what happens when Paradise Regained turns out to be still outside of the Garden wall? When some of those desirable attributes start to rub our deficiencies the wrong way? When we realize that we didn't marry Everywoman, or Everyman?

No one person can be our "all in all"—as so many songs put it. Our individual completion is found not in ourselves, nor even in one special other, or in our gang of friends, our culture, a similar type of person, our age group, or whatever. Our completion is only to be found in the community of all humanity of all time, and this ultimately can only be understood in relation to God.

Marriage *is* a world unto itself; but then again, so is every parent-child relationship, teacher-student relationship, sibling relationship, client, boss, customer, friend. And don't we hate it when we're treated like just another number?! In a truly human sense, every relationship, every connection between one person and another, is unique.

What happens when she isn't all you were expecting, when he has some pretty strange idiosyncrasies that you failed to notice before, when others begin to look more desirable, when my needs aren't being met and I'm not getting "what I want"?

When we get close enough to see the tinsel intertwined with the shining glory, the clay mixed with gold, what then? Is it time to bail out, to grasp after another vision of glory, to think that perfection is just around the corner, on that billboard, in your colleague, or with some passing stranger? Is it time to check out of that which is dissatisfying and check into some "runner-up" alternatives, some other opposites? Surely they can't be as bad as this!

But that one "Yes!" we said in our wedding vows had hidden within it a thousand "No's."

The grass is always greener on the other side of the fence—until you get there!

We came expecting a sumptuous feast without measure, all laid out and waiting for us to dine. Instead we are handed a hoe and a rake, and shown the way into the back garden. "Better is a dish of vegetables where love is, than a fattened ox and hatred with it" (Proverbs 15:17).

It is not only the two separate individuals in a couple who are undergoing both repairs and development; the relationship itself is sadly lacking. Yes, every marriage is deficient; not only can no other person be your "all in all," but the darkness of sin in all aspects of human society has wreaked havoc in the depths of every soul, and at the base of every relationship.

He may have turned out to be a work in process — and *you* aren't? *She* may not have turned out to be all you dreamed of, but have *you* achieved perfection?

Refreshing Waters

Dig in. Dig down. Grow together. Practice contentment. Look at what's really there, not just at what's missing. Look at yourself—have *you* arrived? The temptation to look elsewhere for satisfaction may, for some people, be a constant thing, for others only occasional. Consider the advice and perspective of the wise of long ago concerning this:

> *Drink water from your own cistern, flowing water from your own well.*
>
> *Should your springs be scattered abroad, streams of water in the streets?*
>
> *Let them be for yourself alone, and not for sharing with strangers.*
>
> *Let your fountain be blessed, and rejoice in the wife of your youth, a lovely deer, a graceful doe.*
>
> *May her breasts satisfy you at all times; may you be intoxicated always by her love.*
>
> *Why should you be intoxicated, my son, by another woman and embrace the bosom of an adulteress?*

*For human ways are under the eyes of the LORD, and he
    examines all their paths.*
*The iniquities of the wicked ensnare them, and they are
    caught in the toils of their sin.*
*They die for lack of discipline, and because of their great
    folly they are lost.*
                                    (Proverbs 5:15–23, NRSV)

We war against the world, the flesh, the devil. We are in a war against all that battles us, against all that battles the work of God in creation, and against all that battles the work of God in salvation.

The world would have us believe that only the here-and-now counts, only what you can feel is real, physical beauty is crucial, life without sex is unthinkable, moral purity pays only when it's convenient, it is good for discontentment to fuel the economy, using sex to bolster sales is great, the wages of sin is relational inconvenience, and that corruption is limited to shady money deals—it's not something that can, and does, happen to the soul.

The flesh tries to convince us that it is indeed the center of the universe, that this relationship should be working for *me*, that settling for less is unthinkable, that looking to and waiting on God for happiness is idiotic, that feeling good right now is crucial, that anything that is truly worthwhile should be free and require no input on my part, that real life is devoid of God and smart people take matters into their own hands and get whatever they can whenever they can by whatever means.

Do not be deceived, God is not mocked; for 'Whatever

*you sow, that's what you'll reap'. If you sow to your own
flesh, you will from the flesh reap corruption; but if you
ow to the Spirit, you will from the Spirit reap eternal life.
So let us not grow weary in doing good, for in due
time we **will** reap if we do not give up.*
(Galatians 6:7–9, rendering and emphasis mine).

The same apostle also wrote the verse placed at the opening of this chapter: "Godliness with contentment is great gain" (1 Timothy 6:6, NIV).

Despite the clamoring of our flesh and the noisy monotones of the world and the insidious whisperings of the devil, *godliness* (both relational and sexual), *contentment*, *purity*, and *fidelity*—in every thought, word, and deed—is absolutely crucial to

the health and well-being   and growth   and fun
and wonderfulness   and fullness   of real marriage.

The journey from "sex as physical" to "sex as personal" is contrary to the world out there, the flesh within (for some), and the devil. This journey towards true purity of heart may seem to take longer than a lifetime, but the rewards for the traveler are both immediate and long-term, both constant and true throughout — and we do not travel alone.

Biblical Illustrations and Teaching

1. The goodness of marriage is spoken of in 1 Timothy 4:3-4, and is assumed throughout Scripture. How would you explain this goodness to a culture which has decidedly put a firm question mark over marriage?

2. In Proverbs chapters 5 and 7 there are warnings about relational and marital waywardness. Which reasons given against infidelity and moral looseness do you find most convincing? Discuss these with others. What different reasons do various people find more compelling?

3. Read Ephesians 5:3-14. How can we better live as "children of light"? What things mentioned in the above discussion help to "expose" (v. 11) the ways of darkness in our society? Are there other similar things which should be exposed as false or misleading which war against the soul and marriage?

Little Exercises

1. The constant onslaught of the world can make us feel "like a city broken into and without walls . . . a man who has no control over his spirit" (Proverbs 25:28; see also 4:23). What things in particular wage a war of discontentment against your heart and your marriage relationship? Confess these to a trusted confidant and have them pray with and for you concerning these things.

2. Instead of counting the many deficiencies of your spouse, set these aside for the moment, and count his/her positive

points. Move on from these to include aspects which are only "moderate to good," and only then make a short list of deficiencies. Are you really convinced that your life is "hid in Christ" and that you're not missing something vital? Here's a chance to practice gratitude for what good your spouse has, and acceptance of what he/she will never have.

3. Brainstorm about ways in which you could extend more light into your own sphere of influence, into places and relationships and people's lives, opposing the spirit of sexual looseness and confusion of our day, and promoting instead the alternative and true glory of a healthy perspective of sexuality and of marriage.

Chapter 7

Time Out

The Journey from Harassment to Rest

*One handful of rest
is better than
two handfuls of work
& striving after wind.*

Ecclesiastes 4:6 (rendering mine)

The mountain rose up steep in front of us. It was easy to see the path which ran from our feet across the small valley and all the way up to the top of our destination. I ran ahead. But after a short time I felt badly for my traveling companion, so I stopped and waited. As my sister came closer she called out, "It's okay, you can go ahead. You always like to run out in front." I guess after 20 years or so of tromping in who knows how many woods and meadows together she should know! Regardless, I felt bad at such neglect, and determined that we would *walk* together up the steep pathway.

I was born to run. How many times was I reminded that when I was a little boy, I'd wake up early and hit the ground with my feet running? Hmmm, reminds me of a little boy I've seen—and heard!—running around this house!

Born to run and born to climb. If I had my way, I would have *run* up the side of that mountain. How the heights beckoned to me! What would I see, at the top of this, my first mountain?

Good thing I slowed to a walk. What appeared to be the top of yonder mountain turned out to be only an outcrop, hiding the vast distance which lay beyond it to the *real* mountaintop. From where we finally stopped for lunch, we could see that initial rock—far, far below us. We never did make it to the very top that day; darkness began to descend too early for that. But we did see the plateau at the top, and the range of mountains beyond the one we had started to climb. What an unforgettable sight; yes, well worth the climb!

Fine! "Worth the climb." But would it be worth the jog, or the run?

A friend and I swam across a lake one day. We didn't want to wait for the small motorboat to take us across to the camp we were to be staying at, so we decided to swim the mile-and-one-half to the distant shore. Our friends yelled and waved to us from the boat as they went back and forth picking up people and supplies and delivering them to the faraway camp docks.

All went well, until we were a quarter-mile from shore, and my fearless companion—whose idea it was to swim across in the first place, I might add!—suddenly cramped up in both his legs. With no one in sight at that particular time, we had no alternative but for him to roll over on his back, and for me to hold him with one arm while doing a sidestroke of sorts with my free arm and legs.

What felt like years later, we made it to shore. My legs had turned to rubber. I couldn't even stand up. I could barely crawl onto the pebble beach and lie there in the shallow water, waiting for exhaustion to leave, waiting for that normal functioning to return, waiting for those numb legs to stop screaming in pain so I could stagger forth onto dry land.

Funny, it never crossed my mind to run up that cliff-like hill right in front of us. I guess my brain stopped functioning for a moment. Or would that be a silly thing to do—run up a mountain after a numbing swim across a lake?

What do you think?

Would you run up a mountain after barely making it across a lake?

Would you hold your breath for the entire time while waiting for the 150-car train to finally finish chugging by at the railway crossing?

Would you turn the radio up while practicing your trumpet solo and talking on the phone and explaining to your three-year-old daughter the intricacies of constructing her new 1,000- piece Lego castle?

Do you really need a whole chapter on "time out"?

How can I explain to the unconvinced that running three marathon races back-to-back borders (only *borders?*) on lunacy?

If I don't find any Bible verses countering this special brand of lunacy, will you remain unconvinced?

If I do find some Bible verses countering this special brand of lunacy, will it make any difference?

DANGEROUS BEGINNING

I did a dangerous thing the other day. It could have ruined everything. With such a small start to such a large scheme, I could have buried the whole thing deep in sand. Foolish boy! But I did it anyway, it was there to do, there at the beginning, and I made up my mind; I would start at the beginning. This was a radical thought, unlike what most any right-thinking person would do. But there it was, and so I did it.

I began our brand-new "Adult Sunday School" study of Matthew's Gospel with a killer text: Matthew, chapter one, all the verses from one to seventeen.

That's right. We started with the graveyard passage—the genealogy.

All those dead people, listed row upon row, all with mostly unpronounceable names, related to people we never heard of, all at 9:00 A.M. on Sunday morning.

Make your choice: dead people, or a jog up the mountain.

Since a jog up the mountain would kill most of us, especially at 9:00 on a Sunday morning, let's pause for a moment with the dead people (are you with me?).

Pick a name, any name, from this seemingly endless genealogy. I'll chose a fellow by the name of *Abiud* (found in Matthew 1:13). It appears that Abiud has the distinction of being the son of Zerubbabel. Furthermore, as it turns out, he was also the father on a certain Eliakim.

Between the swim across the lake and the jog up the cliff, did or did not this notable character (Abiud, of course) realize how crucially significant was his place in the vast scheme of things? Did he know that he would someday (some four centuries later) achieve everlasting fame and glory simply by being inserted into Matthew's riveting genealogy, just after Zerubbabel, and just before Eliakim?

(What follows is very long, so take a deep breath.)

As he ran, sipping his hot cappuccino and hurrying his herd of speckled and spotted sheep towards the market and rethinking, for the twentieth time, the Torah lesson for that Sabbath, and wondering if the in-laws would like their present for the new house, and how did Rephaiah (not his real name) make out with that sleazy dealer, and how on earth would Eliakim (his son, remember?) survive if he couldn't even get his ABC's (or the Hebrew equivalent, let the reader understand) straight; in the midst of all this, did or did not Abiud realize that some 400 years later he would be dead, with all his preoccupations long forgotten, and only his name would survive; a footnote (of sorts) in the list linking the Coming Messiah of the World to both the Father of the Faith (Abraham) and the Pre-eminent King (David) whose throne the Messiah would take?

Spiritual Exercise #1: Re-read the above paragraph.

Spiritual Exercise #2: Now re-read the same paragraph, using your name instead of Abiud's.

Does the world look any different?

If the world were a car, somebody has lost the brakes. Now, there is only a gas pedal, and the clutch (it's a standard model) can only shift to higher gears.

The world would bid us run faster, swim harder, dive deeper; and never—no, never—slow down to think, to wonder, to face the unthinkable, to kneel before the wonderful.

This form of worldliness is as prevalent, as pervasive, and as common as pollution. It is older, I am sure, than even the time of Abiud. Many monks and hermits, Christian and non-Christian, from before the time of Christ until now, have fled the tumult and the chaos of the world to clear their minds, if not their hearts. Jesus spoke against this madness when he warned his listeners about the anxious rush after everyday necessities which can so easily characterize ordinary life (see Matthew 6:25-34).

All caffeine and no sleep,
makes Jack a shaky boy.
All go and no stop,
makes for a mind-numbing existence.
Some say: "You can't do business from an empty wagon"
no matter how great the wagon looks.
One said: "Man shall not live on bread alone,"
but plenty get by on just crumbs.
(At least, some try. Do you?)

Time out ...
Isn't that a piper's dream?
"Time" is something children used to have.
You can breathe in, but you can't breathe out.

WAR

When the tide is coming in, "those who are not against us are for us." But when the tide is going out, "those who are not for us, are against us."

The tide is going out. The tide is going out on marriage. The war is on. Good, solid, nurturing, up-building, growing, maturing marriages built upon rock-solid faith and dogged obedience and hang-tough hope are no longer what you'd expect to find near at hand and just next door.

Live as you please. Loosen your morals. Busy up your life. Turn the television on. Head out the door. Help others. Don't think about yourself. Get involved. Do the extra ministry at the church. Go the extra mile, and then another, and another, and another.

In this avalanche of ever-shifting distractions, in this earthquake of changing landscapes and disappearing certitudes, one of the most godly decisions you can make is to decide to be married.

Time out.

I don't mean marriage as "a moment," a quick walk down the aisle.

I mean marriage as a way of life.

If you decide to walk in the way of marriage, to enter its hallowed grounds, to delight in its fruits, you will need to take time out;

> time to cultivate its grounds,
> time to get rid of debris,
> time to plan its progress, yes, and even
> time to (again) delight in its fruit.

A garden of any worth takes time. Weeds grow by accident, anywhere, but flowerbeds only appear by design — *your* design.

The war is on. The world, your own flesh (or "sinful nature," as the NIV puts it), the flesh of others, and the powers of darkness converge to ruin all that is godly, all that is good, and all that is an integral and natural part of God's world.

How can you do battle when you have both hands full of work and are consumed with striving after wind (see the opening verse of this chapter, Ecclesiastes 4:6)? How can you do battle when you hardly ever have even an occasional, single handful of rest; if only to take a breath, gain your bearings, and say hello to your friend and companion?

Do you have a choice?

Would you *like* a choice?

We need to count the cost. We need to consult the bottom line.

First, the cost.

INCONVENIENCE

Time out is—if nothing else—totally inconvenient. It is a waste of time. Important things beckon, needy people call, committees require help, projects need to be done, bills need to be paid, the house is never clean for long, the kids never sleep, Grandpa needs a hand; need and opportunity are endless.

Time out, with your mate, is hardly important.

Time out, with your spouse, will only happen if somebody—say, your fairy godmother—drops off an all-inclusive, all-expenses-paid weekend for two at some totally luxury hotel; and, oh yes, she's provided babysitting, too.

Time out with that one person to whom you swore faithful loving-kindness before God and others, this time out will just "happen"—all things being equal— with the regularity of a Lotto win.

Good luck.

Do you realize that you are married to an eternity? Can you fathom how that person with whom you share your most down-to-earth intimate living space is—in relation to the rest of creation—like one of the gods? Do you know that there is no end to the depth of that person, no end to the creativity in those areas of strength, and no one nearer at hand who bears such an uncanny resemblance to the Creator?

Moreover, there is no one so constantly near at hand through whom the Creator may minister to your needs, counteract your deficiencies, expose your false images, and encourage your developing truest self-in-Christ.

Doing the right thing is so inconvenient.

Take ancient Israel's relationship with God, for example. Three times a year, each male was required to leave absolutely everything—his farm, his means of production, his livelihood, his wife, his children, his livestock, his home—and go to join all the other males for the three national religious festivals. The first time they were to gather together (for a week!) to celebrate the Passover, in remembrance of their deliverance from death in Egypt. Seven weeks later they were to celebrate God's provision in the harvest festival (Pentecost). And finally, at the end of the year, they were again to celebrate God's provision in the festival of ingathering of produce—for yet another week!

God is the cosmic time-waster. How can anyone center life upon the material world, or upon the loftier goal of "love thy neighbor," when the Creator-God constantly demands to be the center of all things — yes, even the center of our affections, projects, committees, marriages, families, neighborhoods, churches and societal structures?

Back to Chapter One. Point #1: *Marriage*: It's Not about You. It's about God.

Building upon that foundation, it's also about your spouse. But not just your spouse — it's about you and your spouse *in relationship* with each other.

No quality without quantity. You have to put in the time. And what will happen if you take time out, if you put in the time marriage requires? Sometimes, nothing happens. At other times you redefine the universe and work out a few possible examples. Regardless, all these things take time.

Being together creates value. Being together deepens relationship.

"But what on earth do you do?" so many people ask me.

Do what you enjoy. Converse about what concerns you. Pray about all things. Go for a walk. Enjoy a dinner. Build some castles in the air. Dream. Scheme. Sort out some problems. Air out some differences. See things from another perspective. Fix things that aren't working as smoothly as you'd like. Figure out some new means of achieving old goals. Admit to new goals; are they workable now, or later, or maybe never?

Leave space for silence. Like the motion of sunlight upon the leaves, everything doesn't have to bear discernible fruit; everything doesn't have to have an immediate and obvious outcome. After all, "one does not always come away from time spent with a friend with a plan or a conclusion" (Padovano, 148). Inner growth, and relational growth, occur at their own rate, often without awareness; but the results will become evident in time.

Time with spouse, like time with God, seems to be a waste. But neither is. And the more time you invest, constantly, and at regular intervals, the greater the cumulative effect.

So much for the cost.

And what is the "bottom line"?

NECESSITY

Aside from opportunity, there is necessity.

After the swim, and the numbing rescue, we pause. Truly, after a grueling ordeal, you have no choice. After the jog up the mountain, you stop for "the pause that refreshes."

Jesus had sent the disciples out two by two. They had traveled without bread, bag, or money. Armed with only the staff in their hands, the sandals on their feet, and the tunic on their backs, they visited place after place proclaiming that all should repent, casting out demons, and curing many who where sick. They returned exalting—and exhausted!

The place where they reconnected with Jesus was so busy with people coming and doing, they couldn't even have a bite to eat.

So Jesus ordered a time out. And they took it (see Mark 6:31-32).

A number of times during the stresses and temptations of his public ministry, Jesus would slip away to a deserted place, often to pray. He did it after he began his public work, when the crowds had been wowed by his teaching, exorcisms, and healings (see Mark 1:35; Luke 4:42). He also did it habitually as his popularity continued to grow (see Luke 5:16).

If the Son of Man—who changed world history in a few brief years in his early thirties—took time out to clear his brain and reconnect with his heavenly Father, how much more so do we need to take time out?

Of course, you say, I know I need time out with God. But isn't this supposed to be a book about marriage?

I'm glad you asked that question. And if you haven't been convinced as yet, consider the following.

"Do two walk together unless they have made an appointment?" (Amos 3:3, NRSV). A proverbial question spoken to God's estranged people, as he desperately tried to convince them to once again walk with their God; and then he would, in turn, walk with them.

Why would you want to walk with your spouse? What is there about walking in peace, in joy, in love, with him,(or with her) that stirs your soul? "Three things are too wonderful for me; four I do not understand," the fourth one being "the way of a man with a girl" (Proverbs 30:18-19, NRSV).

How can I explain the wonder of "together"? I am not such a poet, but poetry would be the closest one could come to expressing the inexpressible.

Do you live together in constant gentleness? Are you generous with one another? Are you kind? Do you look upon one another with the infinite patience of Christ; the One who saw you come into the world, and whose Spirit works and waits for the living seed to grow effectively in your life and character? Are you remarkably self-controlled in all things— in thought, word, and deed—with respect to your spouse?

Are you in every way faithful to this one relationship?

Doesn't God desire these in all relationships? In case you missed it, the things I've woven into the questions listed above are nothing other than the fruit—or the effect—of the Spirit in a person's life; that is, in your each and every relationship.

Yes, and this includes that potentially most intimate of all relationships: marriage.

Are you there yet? Have you arrived? Is there time for confession, for the bringing to light that which impedes your relationship in Christ? Confession, prayer for one another, resolving to change; all these things take—you guessed it—*time*!

Many things necessitate time out:

physical weariness,

busy-ness in caring for others,

the demands of people on your time and energy,

the distance you have to go in your relationship,

the need to regularly rejoice in the goodness of your spouse,

the discipline of gratitude and thankfulness,

the necessity of calling to mind the wonder of that amazing spouse you interact with on a daily basis,

the brevity of this life,

the goodness of God's creation,

the surety of the life to come,

the suffering of the world,

the darkness of the hour,

the frailty of those you love,

the constancy and slyness of the powers against us all,

the confusion which arises so easily in our minds, obscuring our way forward,

our relationships,

our opportunities for service,

and the possibilities of participating vocationally in the wonder of God's created works.

Walk with the one with whom you—in fact—walk. Work it out together. In some fundamental ways — not in every conceivable way, but in some very basic and crucial ways — the two of you complement one another. You're both better off being together. Moreover, I might add, so are we—those who see you "at a distance."

The more the two of you can get yourselves sorted out and progressing forward, not only will you enter into more of God's blessing yourselves, not only will your dependants and intimates and friends be better off, not only those nearby, but also those far away may well share in some of the overflow.

For the common good, for the good of Christian and non-Christian alike, for the good of the Kingdom of God, for the good of the Church of Jesus Christ wherein you fellowship and worship, for the good of any and all who—rightly or wrongly—look up to you (regardless of your awareness of them), for the good of your health, for the good of your soul, for the wonderfulness of your relationship — take time out. A regular, consistent, custom-fitted, affordable, positive time out.

Time out, together.

STRATEGIC RETREATS: WHERE HAVE WE BEEN?

This would be a good place to start.
Where?
Right here, where you are.
There is no other place from which you can do it.

We have been taking "time out" since we were first married. At the time of this writing, that's over eighteen years. Not a lot, but not nothing. We have taken time out before kids and after kids, while living on a shoestring, while being not-yet-missionaries, while living on three different continents, with family near and far, in times of feeling lost and in times when all was clear, in sickness and in health, in times of little and in times of prosperity, when hard-pressed for a five- minute break in a six-week period, and when things have flowed along nicely with lots of time and space around them. In all these variable situations and events, we have done the hard thing; we have persisted in taking the time. And we have reaped the benefits!

Usually we go away somewhere. A change of scenery helps us to relax, unwind, and to get into the mind-set of seeing things anew. A refreshed body helps to refresh the mind and renew the spirit. The amount of money we spend is completely a reflection of what we have—or don't have—to spend.

This isn't a "dreamboat" getaway; this is not a second honeymoon. It is a *strategic* retreat.

When I was a student, we had a new professor join the seminary. His first official appearance was to speak at the faculty-student retreat. He was a famous preacher, and indeed, Preaching was the subject he would be teaching us. So we expected a treat. We were not disappointed.

Since I was in third year at that point, I could appreciate his incredible technique. In fact, a child could appreciate it, it was so evident.

He spoke about "Strategic Retreats."

Actually, he didn't tell us for the longest time what he was going to talk about. All he kept saying, in that early address, was, "Looking back over all my years of ministry, if there was one thing I would change, it would be ..." and then he'd leave us dangling, waiting to hear what that "one thing" would be, while he went on to yet another story which led us back to that "one thing" he would change, if he could.

That one thing that he would change, looking back over all those years, was taking "strategic retreats."

An hour a week, a day a month, a week every year; that's what he would have changed.

He would have built into his life. He would have taken time out.

You need time to pull back from the press and concerns of the urgent and immediate. Time to recall where you've been. Time to think about where you're going. Time to evaluate: Are there things that are going well, which we want to ensure keep going well? Are there things which need to be changed? If so, what changes should we put into place?

Time to be together, with no specific agenda, other than having this time together.

In the beginnings of our relationship, I mentioned this sermon, and this concept, to Sarah. The idea sounded good, so from the very beginning of our married life, we have taken time out, we have gone on "strategic retreats."

Let me clarify something. Although I mentioned it above, it bears repeating: These times are not simply "honeymoons," done over and over again. These are strategic times. It is strategic for us to go away, to hang out, to relax, to enjoy slow dinners and breakfasts together—over which much of our most "strategic" thinking and reflecting takes place.

The ideal for us is four times a year. Due to the variables of life and responsibilities, we've often resorted to three times per year. We've found that two nights away is pretty minimal; the times we've done a "one-nighter," we end up feeling like we've barely arrived, and then it's time to turn around and go home. Three nights away works best for us. More than three is not good as far as the kids are concerned, but they can live with—or at least, they've learned to live with—our absence for those four days and three nights. We are definitely better parents for having been away.

Since I am a very goal-oriented person, I generally take some time during, or towards the end of, our time away to jot down the results of our discussions. I'd note things we've decided to do, things we've decided against, things to continue, times and schedules to rearrange, relationships to pursue, practices to change — all kinds of things.

I've learned to be flexible with goals. After all, the important things in life are to advance in loving God (the first commandment) and loving neighbor (the second). There's no sense in harming the relationship with your "near" neighbor— that is, your spouse—in the name of achieving even the loftiest and noblest of goals, worthy as they may be.

And what do you stand to gain from consistently and habitually "wasting" your time on such retreats?

The profit includes such things as enjoying an increase of personal warmth and harmony; gaining a sense of direction; working on an action plan; discerning what's meaningful; receiving direction and blessing as God ministers to and through and in the midst of your time together; renewing your wonder and appreciation of each other and of God's work in your lives; and seeing your lives anew in the context of the greatness of God's creation and the mystery of his redemptive work in and through his Church.

Begin where you are; let the process develop. Don't doubt that good can come, or even something better. Your relationship is as custom-made as each of you are as individuals: "Work out your own salvation with fear and trembling; for it is God who is at work in you, enabling you both to will and to work for his good pleasure" (Philippians 2:12–13, NRSV).

Time out is time spent together in God's presence. It's never a waste, and always—in the long run—truly effective. Sow time into your marriage today, and you'll reap your reward tomorrow, if not—as is often the case—today as well.

Biblical Illustrations and Teaching

1. Consider the economic and social inconveniences of the yearly feasts prescribed in Deuteronomy 16:1-16. In what ways has God prodded you to take time with him which may be both inconvenient and disruptive? Discuss what your life revolves around, and whether some of these things should continue to occupy center stage.

2. In Mark 6:30-34 and 45–46, we see Jesus calling his disciples aside for a break from their successful completion of a job "well done" and the chaos of their current situation. Are you willing to, and do you, respond to similar invitations for much-needed time out ? Why or why not?

3. In Matthew 11:28-29, Jesus issued a general call for any who are weary and heavily burdened. How might a regular time out together help you to respond to such an

invitation? What obstacles might you anticipate? How could you work on these, so that you may be less impeded in your spiritual life?

Little Exercises

1. Are you convinced of the need for taking time out as a couple? Why or why not? What arguments in the above chapter did you find compelling? Which ones did you find completely unconvincing? Discuss these with your spouse. Are there needs or opportunities you haven't thought of which may merit your time and attention?

2. Take some time out with your spouse. Try a few of them! Discuss some of the things in this chapter you like, or dislike, and why (if you can think of it). Are you deliberate about having time together, or does it happen only by chance? How might not having deliberate time together endanger the health of both yourselves as individuals and your relationship?

3. Regardless of how convinced you are, purpose to take at least three separate times of strategic retreats. Note and discuss the process before, during, and after. After the three, can you see any advancement, or benefit? Can any of those near at hand see benefit?

Chapter 8

WAG THE DOG

The Journey from Slave to Servant

Wives, submit to your husbands.
Ephesians 5:22, NIV

Here's a word of instruction which certainly wasn't penned in the twenty-first century! Some of the concerns and issues which 'submission' raises today were mentioned earlier (see Chapter One, "Same Coin ... Different Side"). Now is the time to look more closely at this passage, so we begin with the obvious question.

What does it mean to *submit?*

Amazing! The passage doesn't say!

This could turn out to be a very short chapter! There's virtually nothing in these two related verses (Ephesians 5:22–23) to help us understand what it means for a wife to submit to her husband.

There are many helpful things which can be learned from the larger setting of these verses. This word to the wives is a part of an instruction to both husbands and wives (see 5:22-33). This husband-and-wife pair is the first of three paired relationships discussed; the second being children and parents (6:1-4), and the third—slaves and masters (6:5-9). The instructions given to these three groups are joined almost seamlessly to the preceding teaching to "be filled with the Spirit" (5:18). All of this is a part of the second half of the entire letter to Ephesians, beginning at the fourth chapter with the exhortation to "live a life worthy of the calling you have received" (4:1, NIV). The entire section has to do with how to live as a Christian.

Almost all of the others spoken to in these paired groups—husbands, children, parents, slaves, and masters—have more explanation or details given than the wives do. The children are told to be obedient to their parents (a more specific directive than that given to the wives, but also without any qualifying considerations included—just a note about their being "rewarded" in some unspecified way). Servants are likewise told to be obedient, with more detail pointing out that in reality, it was Christ they were serving, and that they would receive back from him for any good thing done.

Much more detail is given to the other half of these pairs; the fathers were not to provoke the children, the masters were to give up threatening, and the husbands were to love their wives as Christ does the Church. We already looked at some of the significance of the exhortation to the husbands above, in Chapter One.

What we need to do now is to step back from this passage and consider more fully what was being said, what was left unsaid, some of the implications we may draw concerning the situation back then, and the significance that all of this may have for women today.

At One Time, This Was Clear ...

After two thousand years of church teaching, it's hard to read these verses and pause long enough to picture why these directions needed to be given in the first place. As a general rule, it seems pretty reasonable to assume that no command is given unless needed. So it would appear that back then, it was not uncommon for Christian masters to threaten their servants, presumably in good conscience, and with what we can only guess! Christian fathers would deliberately—or just habitually—provoke their children to the point of anger. Christian husbands would be calmly living with their wives without a thought to "loving" them in any special way. All of this must have passed as just ordinary behavior. And all of this needed to change with the coming of Christianity into everyday lives and home relationships.

The fact that this "word to the wives" was directed *to* the wives must mean that at the time of writing, *they*, at least, understood what this meant for them! After all, it was directed to them, not to their husbands concerning them, as if it was something which needed to be explained! The wives are being treated here as capable of understanding and acting upon this instruction. Although it *was* customary in those days for the man to be in charge of the household, there was also some variation with respect to what freedom a wife might enjoy—either in running the house, or in doing outside endeavors. In this passage, at least, the women are being treated as capable and responsible, able to understand and act upon the directive as given to them.

Since what was intuitively obvious and clear for the original wives and listeners of this letter is not as clear to us as twenty-first century readers, we need to note a number of things in connection to this word to the wives. We'll need to take note of the general tone of the letter in which this directive was given to the wives. We also need to explore what natural limits there may be to this generalized instruction. Following that, we'll look at what other teaching and situations in the New Testament may help us to understand the meaning of this instruction for wives to submit to husbands.

KEEPING WITH WHAT'S CLEAR NOW

It is highly unlikely that the meaning of "submission," being joined with the term "head" throughout Ephesians 5:22–24, could be contrary to the spirit and tenure of the rest of this letter.

From the fourth chapter of Ephesians onward, there are many virtues set forth, all as part of explaining how one should live as a Christian. The kind of Christian character and activity outlined includes such things as:

humility, gentleness, patience,
the inclusiveness of the entire church in growing together,
speaking truthfully, building up others,
and displaying the fullness of the Spirit by spiritual
conversation and songs and in the giving of thanks.

No husband with his wife, parent with a child, or master with a slave was to move outside of any of these things in fulfilling the specific directives given to them for "walking in love" (5:2), even with respect to anyone in this specifically paired kind of relationship.

Moreover, no husband, in reading this directive, could in good conscience turn to his wife and "lord it over her," treating her in an authoritarian manner, based on this and other passages in the New Testament. At different times, both elders (see 1 Peter 5:3) and the apostles (while disciples in training – see Matthew 20:25) needed to be instructed and reminded not to "lord it over" those who were under them. Obviously this is a temptation for some, perhaps many, in positions of authority. What was true then is certainly the case now, too! Those in authority can tend to abuse their position. However natural it may be to use authority in this way, as far as Scripture is concerned, lording it over another person is wrong; it is a misuse of authority.

More specifically, the focus of the function of the husband as "head" in Ephesians 5 is on *cherishing* and *nurturing* his wife. Regardless of how autocratic the society of that time allowed the husband to be in his own home, as far as this particular Christian teaching was concerned, lording it over another—and in this case, the wife—was simply out of the question.

Obviously, domination and control and demanding obedience are not options for any Christian in any place of authority.

This does not do away with authority as such. But it does do away with authoritarianism. Christ, husbands, parents and masters (one could think of employers) still have authority, but the goal of Christian authority is to serve, not to be served. The conduct and character of Christ is to be always before us in whatever sphere of authority we have—as a model, an example, a goal and a guide for our own attitudes and responses.

How Shall Christians "Fill in the Blank"?

A second thing which can be noted in connection with this general directive to wives is a danger for successive generations of readers. It is tempting to read into this general passage more detail than it provides on its own. Women have had a variety of places and roles in different societies throughout history. This ancient passage does not give anything more than a generalized directive. There is no hint of what to do in the case of unbelieving or abusive husbands, or even concerning those who would force their wife(s) into illegal, immoral, or anti-Christian activities—like sacrificing to other gods, according to the imperial order of Caesar (Best, 524-527, 538).

In leaving this passage—and many others like it—to the Church, perhaps it is God's desire not to give us a set of explicit instructions which cover every conceivable situation. It may be that God desires us to struggle through the difficult process of interpretation, knowing that both the journey and the destination of this process are integral parts of our growth, both individually and collectively over time. Working together with other Christians, within a variety of situations, opportunities and challenges, may well be part of a deliberate plan God set in motion in leaving us the New Testament as it is. How normal it is for students to want only the answer to a particular question; whereas a good teacher desires the student to struggle, to *become* wise, not just to note more information, to make one good decision, or to gain only one noteworthy insight.

The open-ended nature of this passage—as with many passages—left subsequent generations of Christians to struggle in understanding how it applies to them. In this day, in the twenty-first century, women are a part of the process of determining the meaning and implications of this passage for Christians today—and that reality is part of what is new in modern interpretation.

Even within the New Testament, it was expected that situations would arise which would necessitate the distilled wisdom and judgment of the leaders and qualified people within the community. In the early Church, the apostles and the elders, along with the whole church, came together to deliberate on a crucial issue: whether or not non-Jews needed to undergo the rite of circumcision in order to become true Christians (see Acts15:6). Concerning a specific church which seemed to have more than its fair share of problems, Paul asked why the believers were taking each other to court, and that before unbelievers: "Can it be that there is no one among you wise enough to decide between one believer and another" (1 Corinthians 6:5, NRSV).

What I am saying is this: We cannot *always* look to Scripture for something pre-packaged – *the* specific answer to *our* every problem. Nor can we expect instant clarity in how to apply its generalized directives and principles in our every situation. The meaning and implications of Scripture are in part mediated by the ongoing work of the Spirit of God in and through his people, beginning within the New Testament itself. Every Christian is a part of this process. Even though the weight of consideration must obviously go to the distilled considerations of the (hopefully) wise and learned involved in the larger discussion, no one person is free from the struggle to understand and apply the truths and teachings of Scripture to the concrete realities of everyday situations and relationships.

Absolute or General Guidelines?

Most rules, commands and instructions have some built-in limit. Usually these are understood and often they are unspoken; and usually it is only those who are new to a situation who don't know the natural limits and boundaries of general procedures and guidelines.

I tell the kids to look both ways before crossing the street. This is a sensible way to avoid an untimely death. But what if the street is closed for a street market? Well, then we can just walk off the curb without stopping to check for cars. Do I outline all the mundane or possible exceptions when giving my directives? Hardly! I'll just be happy when this little safety rule becomes an automatic reflex for them. Spelling out all possible and hypothetical situations may do for lawyers in their endlessly-worded documents, but it hardly makes sense for everyday conversation.

In most emergencies we depart from normal, routine behavior. People don't normally stand in the middle of a highway frantically waving their arms, unless there's been a fresh accident and they need to stop oncoming traffic! A change of circumstances often brings about a change of the "rules" which apply; this is common sense.

In Ephesians 6, there are directives for masters and slaves. For the most part there are no such positions today, at least in the Western world. But these exhortations can easily be applied to similar situations, such as employers and employees. Such an application is hardly straining the passage much at all; our situation has changed, but the relationship of master-slave is similar enough to the workplace that the instructions to the one group are applicable to the other. Indeed, with the poor on the one hand, and greedy or thoughtless "bosses" on the other, such an exhortation is virtually timeless, even though the specific relationship of master-slave is no longer a part of most societies.

What this means, concerning the submission of wives to husbands, is that this one instruction needs to be read alongside of other such instructions. Only in this way can we see what might have been the natural limits and the understood boundaries of this kind of passage.

SPHERES OF SUBMISSION

How should Christians respond to those in varying positions of authority? In Romans, Paul says, "Let every person be in subjection to the governing authorities....there is no authority except from God, and those which exist are established by God....rulers are not a cause of fear for good behavior, but for evil....[they] are servants of God, devoting themselves to this very thing" (13:1, 3, 6; NIV uses "submit" in place of "subjection," as it does in Ephesians 5:21-24). This was written during the time of the Roman Empire, which was not exactly a just system of government, above reproach in every way!

On the other hand, we see the apostles Peter and John talking back to the religious authorities who had commanded them not to speak or teach in the name of Jesus. To that directive for silence the apostles replied, "Whether it is right in the sight of God to give heed to you rather than to God, you be the judge; for we cannot stop speaking what we have seen and heard" (Acts 4:19-20).

The first directive to submit to governing authorities points in the direction of the ideal response to, and function of, any authority, all things being equal. From time to time all things are *not* equal, and something else must been done. Judgment and discernment must be exercised.

Paul certainly did not submit to the "false brethren" (Galatians 2:4) who came preaching "a different gospel" (1:6). As he later recounted, "We did not yield in subjection to them for even an hour" (2:5). Instead, he opposed Peter "to his face" (2:11) when he saw that the whole group was acting hypocritically and not in keeping with the gospel (see 2:11-14). Paul's regard for James, Peter and John—reputed pillars of the church (see 2:6)—was subject to their own keeping to the truth of the gospel. In fact, this was a standard he applied to himself as well: "Even if we or an angel from heaven should proclaim to you a gospel contrary to what we proclaimed to you, let that one be accursed" (1:8, NRSV).

Not only were Christians expected not to subject themselves to a false gospel, they were not expected to submit themselves even to a true apostle who preached a false gospel!

This is the same Paul who could say to another group of believers, "Just as you have always obeyed, not as in my presence only, but now much more in my absence, work out your salvation with fear and trembling" (Philippians 2:12). Paul expected to be obeyed, just as the other New Testament writers did. The New Testament is full of imperatives, not just suggestions!

There was authority assumed in both the declaration of the gospel and in the implications it had for believers and unbelievers alike. However, as the previous passages made clear, there are limits to political, religious, or even apostolic, authority! All human authority—in any sphere—is a relative authority. These authorities were, and are, real. We owe them due respect and allegiance. But they are not absolute.

By implication of a variety of New Testament passages, the husband, too, was under authority. His authority, in the context of marriage, is also a relative authority. Both the husband and the wife are to be subject to the authority of other believers. This would include the elders or spiritual leaders (see 1 Peter 5:1-5). This would also include the entire Church (see Matthew 18:15-20), all of whom were to be in keeping with the gospel and its implications as it has been given to us through the Scriptures.

SISTER, LET ME BE YOUR SERVANT

For the wife to submit to her husband means that she is submitting to a relative authority. She, like her husband, has already submitted to the absolute authority of God, and to Christ; and like her husband she is also submitted to the relative authority of the church.

The relative authority of the church includes its various spiritual leaders, such as the apostles, prophets, evangelists, pastors and teachers mentioned in Ephesians 4:11. These people had been given the authority to serve. They did not have as their mandate the subjugation of those under them. They were not there to be self-serving. They were there to enable the growth of the church. They are not the head of the church, to whom each individual member of the church is expected to cling (see Colossians 2:19). Rather, they help to equip all to grow in Christ, as it is spelled out in the following passage:

*We are to grow up in all aspects **into Him**, who is the head, even Christ, from whom the whole body, being fitted and held together by that which every joint supplies, **according to the proper working of each individual part**, causes the growth of the body for the building up of itself in love.*

(Ephesians 4:15–16, emphasis mine)

The centre of the relationship between husband and wife is God. The source of their relationship, as for all Christians, is Christ. To the workings of God the Father, Son and Spirit, both husband and wife are to be submitted, individually and together. The context of their relationship is their ongoing involvement with, and submission to, the many different ministries found within the Body of Christ.

Regardless of how autocratic the society of that time allowed him to be in his own home, the authority of the husband has been severely reconfigured in this Ephesians passage to focusing on the nurturing and nourishing of his wife—modeled on the self-sacrificial example of Christ.

A related picture of service for the husband is that of Christ in John's Gospel (see 13:1-17). There we find Jesus with a towel wrapped around him, washing the disciples' feet. In this fashion the husband is to love his wife. And if the wife refuses to submit to such service, it is like Peter not wanting his Lord to stoop so low—like a common servant!—in order to wash his feet.

The goal of the husband's service to the wife is her spiritual health and general well-being. I think that the situation is similar to the general exhortation given to Christians in Hebrews 13:17: "Obey your leaders, and submit to them; for they keep watch over your souls, as those who will give an account." In fact, all of us should be grateful for any who have a sincere concern for the state of our souls, and should respond with ready acceptance to the insights and admonitions which such may give to us for our good.

But He's So Imperfect!

What if the husband doesn't measure up? What if the wife is married to an unbeliever, or someone who behaves worse than even most unbelievers? How far should one take this directive to submit to one's husband?

Many commentators on the Ephesians 5:22-24 passage point out that the submission here is a "voluntary" submission. That is, it was given to the wives to voluntarily continue to submit to their husbands, as was normal in their society. Many also point out the "ideal" nature of what is envisioned in this passage, a Christian wife and a Christian husband, with nothing said about any major issues which may be ruining the relationship or the people involved.

One's given condition in life is not one's position for all eternity. In 1 Corinthians, Paul states a general principle which applies to this: "Let each of you remain in the condition in which you were called" (7:20, NRSV). It would appear that at that time and place there was some sort of distress the Corinthian believers were facing (see vv. 26, 29). So Paul said that slaves were not to worry about being slaves; but if they could become free, of course it would be better to do that (see v. 21).

In that circumstance, Paul was urging people to remain as they were: whether married, single, circumcised, uncircumcised, free, or enslaved. He directed that an unbelieving spouse should be able to stay if they wish (see vv. 12- 16), for this would sanctify the children who would also stay, and indeed the spouse might become a believer. But if a wife left her husband, she should return, or remain unmarried, and the husband should not leave his wife (v. 11).

In light of that distressful time, it was generally better to stay put, and not seek to change status or position. One thing that is remarkable about this passage is the relative freedom presupposed of the believers, even with respect to marriage. A distressing circumstance, a state of emergency, could alter the regard for the looseness or the tightness of the marriage bound.

This could be another example of a natural logical limit to normal relationships and functioning. If the house was burning down, everyone would help everyone out of the building; normal relationships become temporality suspended because of the crisis at hand.

There are other times when relationships are strained over a longer period, when there is more than just a short-lived emergency. In 1 Peter we read more instructions for slaves and wives:

> *Servants, be submissive to your masters with all respect, not only to those who are good and gentle, but also to those who are unreasonable....In the same way, you wives, be submissive to your husbands ... even if any of them are disobedient to the word.*
>
> (1 Peter 2:18; 3:1)

The hope expressed here is that the husband may be won through the behavior of his Christian wife.

Is there a natural logical limit to these directives to wives in Ephesians? I would think so. Extreme circumstances may call for an alteration of what is normal; but even this should be in accordance to the general guidelines given to us in Scripture. Moreover, such decisions should be determined in consultation with spiritual leaders, elders and pastors, with an eye to the wider thought and discussion of Christians throughout the history of the Church.

What I'm saying here seems out of keeping with the kind of pastoral involvement that I've seen, or rather *not* seen, between most church folk and the elders or spiritual leaders in a church community. Too often there is missing some sort of mechanism, or relationship, in place so as to air grievances between couples and sort out what makes good sense and what doesn't.

Just as Moses had help in bringing justice to the vast number of the Israelites, putting qualified people in charge of thousands, hundreds, fifties and tens (see Exodus 18:17-23), so a community can set up helpers at different levels, or at least have select people, to help smooth the nagging differences which can arise within a marriage. Extreme situations can be brought before the congregation, if attempts on the individual level have failed (see Matthew 18).

All of this is to say that submission to one's husband is not an absolute condition, nor is marriage a suicidal short road to becoming a nonentity for the wife. If the husband is devoted to loving his wife, to nourishing and cherishing her, in the self-sacrificial manner of Christ, seeking her own interests above his own (as we are directed to do in Philippians 2:3-5), and with a concern for her soul, then I would think that most wives would willingly submit to such dedication and devotion. Again, all the virtues mentioned in Ephesians (chapters 4–6) can come into play here, characterizing both husband and wife, at least as goals they're working towards.

In the case of an abusive or negligent husband, a wife may elect to stay, for the good of the children or the hope of winning the husband to Christ. In such cases, though, she should certainly be enlisting the help of elders and others to advocate for change in the situation. In extreme cases, I don't see how submitting to a debilitating or dangerous spouse can be in keeping with any Scripture. We must not use general directives for ordinary life as though these were tyrannical laws devoid of compassion and blind to extreme situations. Even Paul, in addressing the situation in 1 Corinthians 7, wrote his instructions in order to spare them from trouble, to free them from concern, for their benefit, and for their happiness (see 7:28, 32, 35, 40).

God has provided for both ordinary and extraordinary situations. Our submission to him, and to his various means of grace, is for our good and our benefit, both individually and collectively. There can be no set of complete answers given beforehand which cover every situation; but we have the Spirit and the gifts, and we have Scripture and the cumulative advice and reflection of the wise and learned, both past and present. Moreover, God is present in all situations, so we have hope of his guidance even through ways which seem dark and confusing.

THE HEAD WHO SERVES

With the coming of Christianity, it was actually the husband who lost considerable "power." In the general society of the first century, the man had the say in his own house. Nothing would have been easier for the New Testament writers than to affirm this high and rather exclusive position of power.

Furthermore, the term "head" is used a number of times with reference to Christ's being over all authority. Colossians 2:10 states that "[Christ] is the head over all rule and authority," and Ephesians 1:22 says that "[God] put all things in subjection under His [Christ's] feet, and gave Him as head over all things to the church."

But in reference to how both Christ and the husband are supposed to *function*, the emphasis falls not on their exercise of authority as much as their being a *source* of love and life. Christians are "to grow in all aspects into Him, who is the head, Christ, *from whom* the whole body ... causes the growth of the body for the building up of itself in love" (Ephesians 4:15 - 16, emphasis mine; see also Colossians 2:19).

Likewise in Ephesians 5:22-33, as we have already seen, the role of the husband is to nurture and cherish his wife. Moreover, the enlisting of Christ as the example emphasizes his saving role: "The husband is the head of the wife, as Christ also is the head of the church, He Himself being the *Savior* of the body" (Ephesians 5:23, emphasis mine).

Although Christ has the position of head over the Church, which includes being head over all rule and authority, his relationship to the Church is that of a source of life. He *gives* to the Church, and each part is to cling to him. This is the model, example, and explanation of "headship" found in the New Testament.

Although the society had given the husband the role of authority over the wife, these teachings turn that role into one of service for the good of his spouse! The "head" still had its place of authority, but that authority was now to act as a source of life for those under its charge.

The submission of the wife is, in the best of worlds, a submission to love. This is not some romantic kind of love; although that isn't necessarily excluded, but it isn't necessarily included, either. The goal of this love is modeled on the *activities* of Christ. This included cleansing the Church from sin, and eventually presenting her without spot or wrinkle, holy and blameless (see Ephesians 5:26-27). This activity is related to the constant command throughout the New Testament for believers to turn from evil and do good, or from darkness to light. The husband has a responsibility to help his wife in this process of ever becoming more Christian.

Headship turned on its head; this is such a typical way of God reversing the values and practices of the world—reversing them back to reflect his own values and practices. Even submission is reversed, from being a potential "slave" status determined by societal expectations, to being a "servant" status—a freewill offering by the woman herself to God, Christ, and her husband. This frees her from submitting to what could "naturally" be a source of abasement or humiliation to submitting to what was destined to become a source of love and nurture and support. How hard it is to continue to be Christ-like in working out what these things mean in our everyday lives and relationships; but by his grace and our perseverance we can become ever more Christian, even in our closest and most constant relationships.

Biblical Illustrations and Teaching

1. In John 20:5–17, we see Jesus washing his disciples' feet. In what ways do you think husbands do, or should, serve their wives? How much are these ways solely functional? How many are more relational? How many are more spiritual?

2. In what ways would you find it difficult to "obey your leaders, and submit to them" (Hebrews 13:17)? How do you see obedience, submission, and leadership working out in the home situation? What are some ways you can improve on these to help your spiritual progress and growth?

3. In Matthew 18:15-20 we read that if our "brother" (or sister) sins, we are to reprove him in private. How do you deal with sin in the life of your spouse? At what point do you think one should enlist the help of others in reproving a spouse? How would such an action help, or harm, those involved, or the relationship itself?

Little Exercises

1. Take turns submitting to one another — maybe for a day, or for an entire week. Purpose to be willing to lay aside whatever you had planned, and go along with the other person's preferences. How willing are you to turn from what you want to do? How willing are you to take the lead and make the final decisions? Discuss these dynamics. What do they teach you about your Christian

character, either in general or in the specific relationship of marriage?

2. Ask your spouse for one specific thing you can do which may help you become more Christian. Even if you don't understand how this thing makes sense, try putting this activity into practice — perhaps for two weeks, or maybe for a whole month. Discuss this process with some trusted friends. Is there something you should be changing on a more permanent basis?

3. List the ways in which you find it difficult to "submit yourselves for the Lord's sake to every human institution" (1 Peter 2:13). What do you think you will be losing by such submission? How might reluctance in this area be affecting your general ability to submit in more important areas?

Chapter 9

KIDS: PART OF THE PACKAGE

The Journey from War to Remembrance

Children are a gift from the LORD. . . .
How blessed is the man whose quiver is full of them.
Psalm 127:3, 5 (rendering mine)

A man's enemies will be the members of his household.
Matthew 10:36

Tension. You can feel it rolled up tight in the pit of your stomach. The silence grows deeper. From another room you can hear the giant stirring, pacing, muttering. Barely breathing, you wonder: *With all that pressure building, when will the volcano explode?* With lava flying everywhere, hot words scorching, shredding, with thunderings which shake the very foundations.

The parent loses it. The child gets it. There's fallout everywhere.

Really, it wouldn't have happened if it weren't for that son, that daughter. What she said! What he does!

Question: Did that son really create all that buildup? Was it solely because of that daughter's behavior that you lost it—so very badly?

SUNRISE, SUNSET

For some people, children are the long-awaited blessing. They delight in infants, kids, and even teenagers! The entire process of having kids, from childbearing to the coming of grandchildren, is one of joy.

This is a pleasant scenario. It is reminiscent of the very human desire expressed in ancient Israel, and in our society it is still a mythological and cultural ideal. It is the stuff of TV commercials and family-oriented shows. It sounds so good, and it looks even better. Perhaps you too wish this reflected your own family experience, either what you grew up with, or what you presently now have. I certainly wish it had reflected mine.

Indeed, for other people, children are more like a "mixed blessing." Sometimes things are good; there is peace and order, excitement in living, growth and development, hope for the future. At other times—moments, long hours dragging by, days, even weeks, sometimes longer—a darkness descends, as if from nowhere. Chaos erupts, and you're living in a war zone.

The dream of a home all safe and secure can be weak indeed, especially in a world of downsizing and global competition and job uncertainty. To add to this, at any time beyond early childhood, children are exposed (via the media and the Internet) to influences from all over the world; some wonderfully broadening, but others? Ruinous!

Modern media places a great value on computer skill and know-how, often with kids leading the way. The upshot of this is that parents are often placed on a pretty low-playing field; they sometimes have to ask their own kids how these "essential" things work! It's too easy for the young—immature and inexperienced as they are—to begin to think less of those adults who lack their basic technical ability. And to those adults who have some know-how, there is often an attitude of "equality." After all, teenagers typically think they know it all; and now someone has given them the code to worldwide knowledge—what a head trip! As a result, the roles of home have been reordered.

Parental influence and control have been weakened. Job security is a dream. Marriage is reduced to one of several options—"if that's what you like." Home is a building where people who inhabit different worlds occasionally cross paths. In the midst of all of this fragmentation, an "in your face" attitude often prevails among the young towards anybody older who doesn't inhabit their brave new world.

Children are still present, but where do they fit in? In our heart of hearts, how do we see them? Are they indeed a blessing, or do they occasionally—or even constantly—seem more like "the enemy within the gates"?

Against what do we struggle?

Who, or what, is the real enemy?

IN YOUR FACE

In the midst of daily pressures and challenges, with seasonal tensions and sudden flare-ups, the question of "who is my enemy?" begs to be answered with the obvious, flesh and blood "*that* person over there!"-type answer.

"It's *her* fault, *I* didn't do anything!"

"Well, if only *you'd* stop making so much noise . . . you know I can't stand it!"

The petty arguments and disagreements of children. Attack and counterattack. *I'm* innocent, *you're* wrong; you *deliberately* acted that way! Kids and adults may express it differently (sometimes, but not always!), but the underlying hostility is the same.

I've even seen grown adults engaged in the infantile "yes, you did!"/ "no, I didn't!" kind of mindless argument — in public yet! Usually grown-ups engage in such warfare more discreetly: behind closed doors, or in the courtroom.

Kids, on the other hand, aren't so selective; they'll bad-mouth each other virtually anywhere, anytime. Emotions are more raw, survival is at stake, reason is limited, experience is narrow, and the world as they know it is quickly unraveling— right now!

The ill feelings and antagonism which so easily arise in childhood don't necessarily get shed in youth, or even beyond then, in the adult years. We dream of peace, but we live in the midst of war. "I want what I what" is still a basic approach to life; it's our instinctive, fundamental mode of operation. This "I" clings with tenacious power to the controls of our life and our relationships.

What we experience, in the here and now, may appear like face-to-face conflicts. This is the obvious way to read the in-your-face conflicts of family living. When the emotions are aroused, when fear or fury sets in, it's hard to think beyond the apparent, beyond the obvious. We think, "It's *you*," a flesh and blood reality outside of, apart and quite distinct from myself.

VISIBLE FOES, INVISIBLE WARFARE

In striking contrast to this, the apostle Paul said "our struggle is not against flesh and blood" (Ephesians 6:12). In other words, our struggle is *not* against people.

How could Paul say such a thing?! Few people have suffered as he did from real people "out there." Consider the following hardships Paul reported suffering, all of which likely happened within the first twenty years of his conversion. Comparing himself to some false teachers who were pretending to be apostles, Paul recounts how he had suffered far more than they had for the sake of the gospel—a staggering amount, if you read it slowly enough:

> *I have been in far more imprisonments,*
> *beaten times without number,*
> *often in danger of death.*
> ***Five times** I received from the Jews thirty-nine lashes.*
> ***Three times** I was beaten with rods,*
> ***once** I was almost stoned to death, ...*
> *On frequent journeys I've been in danger from robbers,*
> *dangers from my own countrymen,*
> *dangers from the Gentiles ...*
> *dangers from false brethren.*
> (2 Corinthians 11:23–28,
> rendering and emphasis mine)

Many stories of Paul's hardships can be found throughout the book of Acts. But despite all of this obviously very human opposition—from such a great diversity of people—Paul maintained that his struggle was not against "flesh and blood."

Certainly Paul had physical enemies, but he saw that his real enemy was not physical; his real enemy was spiritual. After he declared that "our struggle is not against flesh and blood" (Ephesians 6:12), he went on to explain the real nature of our warfare: "[Our struggle is] against the rulers, against the powers, against the world forces of this darkness, against the spiritual forces of wickedness in the heavenly places" (Ephesians 6:12).

Paul could see that his *real* struggle was a struggle against spiritual forces; it was not against flesh and blood people. The same, of course, can be said about parents and their kids. Kids are not the enemy of the parents. They are not the reason why a husband or a wife may stumble, or why a marriage may grow sour. No one person is our enemy.

Our warfare is spiritual.

STRUGGLES WITHIN

It's easy to understand how we fight against things which would physically harm us. Never before have we been so preoccupied with physical health and well-being! We have worked hard to conquer our environment, minimizing damage from storms and drought and famine. We work just as hard to minimize harm from the microscopic world. Science and medicine are pressed into service not only to rid us of all ills, but also to make our lives as long and pleasant as possible.

But our lives are not merely physical. More profoundly than our animal-like, creaturely lives, we are spiritual beings.

Christians throughout the centuries have maintained that we have three enemies: the world, the flesh, and the devil. As Christians, we are to war against those things which seek to destroy us as spiritual persons. As in the physical world, this includes anything in both the macro and the micro worlds. Here the focus is on things which oppose and are contrary to God. This includes ungodly systems—both local and global—which are "out there" (i.e., the *world*). Just as importantly, it includes all ungodly values and habits which are "in here" (i.e., the *flesh*). The powers of darkness—as in the *devil*—all the while seek to destroy us through both the world and the flesh.

Note: No sign of kids here!

So why does it sometimes seem to be such a struggle to have a consistently good, rock-solid marriage with all these kids running around?

It's not all that difficult to see why! There is a constant barrage of needs which are part-and-parcel of any infant's life. It's not untypical for parents of the very young to practically lose all sense of time; hours blur to days, to weeks, and even to months!

And as the kids grow, often the expectations of parental involvement grow with them. On behalf of the kids, parents busy themselves with meals and parties and clubs and extra lessons and friends; and somewhere in there, even the necessary household chores and projects get neglected. The treadmill never stops until the parent collapses in a heap.

Who has time for marriage?!

Is this a necessary scenario? Is it an either-or situation: *either* a good family life, hale and hearty, *or* a marvelous marriage? (But certainly not both!) Who wouldn't *want* both? But to *have* both is a real struggle!

"So much work, so little time!"

"A man works from sun to sun; but a woman's work is never done." And now it's even worse, since so many woman feel responsible not only to "work under the sun" out there in the marketplace, but also to ensure the home is running well.

Blaming the kids for our inner and relational struggles is like any other way of blaming the environment. It's not my fault—it's *them*. If they didn't exist (*not* an option!) I'd be ok, I'd be sane, I'd be able to cope. It's not me; it's them.

But is it only them? Recall the threesome against which we do battle: the world, the flesh, the devil. Recall my somewhat tongue-in-cheek comment: No sign of kids here!

Where is the real source of struggle? If it's not the kids, could it be one of these three enemies mentioned above?

ROOTS AND FRUITS

James identifies "the source of quarrels and conflicts" as our "pleasures that wage war in [our] members" (James 4:1). This may sound like a far cry from letting off some steam at some unruly kid, but James does a great job of opening up the inner dynamics of our conflicts.

To make use of one of the three terms mentioned above, the source of our inner struggles is to be found in our *flesh*, that is, in our sinful nature (as the NIV often translates the term "flesh"). The source of our struggles is in how we handle our desires—our wants and our wishes.

We would, no doubt, *like* to have the exceptional character that James describes: "Who among you is *wise* and *understanding?* Let him show by his *good behavior* his deeds *in the gentleness of wisdom*" (3:13, emphasis mine). Doesn't this sound like the perfect parent?

James expands on this picture-perfect person, noting both the source, and the outcome, of this sterling character:

> *The wisdom from above*
> *is first pure,*
> *then peaceable,*
> *gentle, reasonable,*
> *full of mercy and good fruits,*
> *unwavering, without hypocrisy.*
> *And the seed whose fruit is right relationships— is sown*
> *in peace by those who make peace.*
>
> (3:17-18, rendering mine)

Wouldn't every parent love to be described in this way?!

Unfortunately, we so easily slip—however momentarily—into a lower form of relating. In contrast to the exemplary, godly behavior described above, James describes this other kind as follows:

> *But if you have bitter jealousy and selfish ambition in*
> *your heart,*
> *do not be arrogant and so lie against the truth.*
> *This wisdom is not that which comes down from above,*
> *but is earthly, natural, demonic.* (3:14-15)

James has again targeted the source of this mindset—it is earthly, natural, and demonic. He also expands on its root, and its fruit:

For where jealousy and selfish ambition exist,
there is disorder
and every evil thing. (3:16)

Two sources, two outcomes. One source is heavenly, "from above," the work of the Spirit; the other source seems almost everyday and ordinary ("earthly, natural"), but its roots are ultimately demonic.

We are a mixture of both.

Hence, our struggle.

BITTER-SWEET

Before his description of these two types of character, James had been describing the use of the tongue, and how disastrous our words can be. Some people think that Christians should automatically be included in the "wisdom from above" description, but notice that James includes even himself among those who use the tongue in both blessing and cursing. What he says there can certainly be applied in how parents can, and often do, converse with their sons and daughters.

With [our tongue] we bless our Lord and Father; and
with it we curse [those] who have been made in the
   likeness of God;
from the same mouth come both blessing and cursing.
My brethren, these things ought not to be this way.
(3:9-10)

Not only has James included himself in saying "these things ought not to be this way," he goes on to point out how impossible this kind of situation is in the created world:

Does a fountain send out from the same opening
   both fresh and bitter water?
Can a fig tree, my brethren, produce olives,
or a vine produce figs?
Neither can salt water produce fresh.
(3:11-12)

But unlike the created world, our inner world is not so well ordered. There is chaos within our souls; we are a mixture of both the heavenly and the "demonic." The discussion about the tongue lead James right on to the broader description of these two spheres of behavior, concerning the wisdom "from above" and the wisdom which is "earthly and demonic."

When Christians say, "We war against the flesh," they are speaking about this kind of struggle. What is the flesh? The flesh is anything in our values and habits—both those inner and those expressed—which is contrary to God and his ways. The flesh shows itself in our actions, speech, or thoughts—whether reactive or deliberate—which is contrary to, less than, or not flowing out of the fullness of a richly developed and mature faith, hope, and love.

Paul saw that our inner struggles are not against people; rather, they are spiritual. James offers a more precise description of where these struggles come from — they come from our own sinful inclinations and desires.

"The kids" are not our enemy, nor are kids the enemy of a fully developed marriage which reaches into the innermost part of who we are as a person and which is blessed to the outermost part of our spheres of influence and life. Our inner struggles are exactly that —inner. We cannot blame those "out there" for what arises and erupts from "in here."

Choosing Your Source

If the kids aren't the cause of our struggles, how then are we to deal with the challenges and inner strain which arise in our ongoing relationship with them? How are we to "do battle" against the enemy within—the flesh? How are we to move from the demonic character which arises from earthly wisdom, to the Christ-like character which comes from the "wisdom from above"?

In showing the way out of these struggles, James actually mentions all three of our classic enemies: the world, the flesh, and the devil. Those whose focus is on getting what *they* want, whose mind is set on their *own* pleasures, he calls "[friends] of the world" (4:4), and "whoever wishes to be a friend of the world makes himself an enemy of God" (4:4, see vv. 1-4).

Regarding the devil, James simply says, "Resist the devil and he will flee from you" (4:7). But how do we resist the devil? How do we turn from being a friend of the world?

We have to choose our source—the source from which our inner life flows. We must choose how we will live: either according to the flesh, or according to the Spirit (see Galatians 5:16). We are to turn from our own pleasure towards God. We are no longer to act out of pride, but we have to declare our submission to, and dependency upon, God. We have to count ourselves amongst those who have "crucified the flesh with its passions and desires" (Galatians 5:24).

The pathway back to God, back to reality, is the pathway of humility. Drawing on a number of Old Testament passages, James says, "God is opposed to the proud, but gives grace to the humble" (4:6; see also Proverbs 3:34 and Psalm 138:6). And after expanding on what's involved in this, James wraps up his thought by repeating again this key and crucial point: "Humble yourselves" (4:10).

As we do an about-face in deliberately submitting to God, we are also to actively "resist the devil" (4:7), instead of resisting the Spirit of God. But we have to move beyond simply turning from evil towards God; we are to "draw near to God," for then "He will draw near to you" (4:8). We need to reconnect with our true source, from whom alone comes the satisfaction of all our desires (see James 1:17).

The source of my struggles is not outside of myself, in circumstances or in people. The source of my struggles is within; my unthinking and automatic focus upon my own desires. I must stop grabbing after what I want, or even what I assume I *need*. Instead of this instinctive "grab what you can" approach, James tells us to "cleanse your hands, you sinners" (4:8).

The very root of our problem is exposed by the next directive: "Purify your hearts, you double-minded" (4:8). In this exhortation, James is harking back to his opening comments in chapter one. There we were told, "If any of you lacks wisdom, let him ask of God....But let him ask *in faith* without any doubting....For let not that man expect he will receive anything from the Lord, being a double-minded man, unstable in all his ways" (1:5–8, emphasis mine).

To trust, or not to trust—that is the crucial question.

If we hesitate, if we are uncertain, if we pull back from trusting God fully, then we will grab for what we can, when we can. We will—however momentarily or occasionally—function like those who have no faith, like those who have no God. We will become unstable in all our ways (see 1:8), in our inner world there will be "disorder and every evil thing" (3:16). We will dirty our hands as those who operate out of selfish ambition, as those who act out of jealousy (see 3:16).

To purify our double-hearts, we need to become single-hearted. I must turn from the mind-set which is *primarily* focused on getting "what I want," which aims above all else to fulfill its heartfelt desires. This situation is the same as what Jesus was getting at when he instructed his followers against being anxious about such basics as food and clothing: "For all these things the Gentiles eagerly seek" (Matthew 6:32). For the follower of Christ, the alternative focus is rather to "seek first [the] kingdom [of God] and His righteousness" (6:33). We need to declare our absolute trust in God, and humbly submit fully to him.

Remember, this is not a onetime effort. The journey may have started with that one step of faith, but it is only carried through with a thousand other steps of faith, of growing and learning, of determining once again to trust him fully.

This may sound like James has pretty well made his point. Stop being friends of the world. Humble yourself and get reconnected to God. Resist the devil. Choose the Spirit rather than the flesh as the mainspring of your life. What more could he say? Isn't it enough, in counteracting our inner struggles to go to war against our friendship with the world, to resist our compliance with the devil, and to clean up our act?

Death before Life

James would have us go one step further. God is, after all, "a consuming fire" (Hebrews 12:29). As a parent can dream of their child's future in ways which exceed a child's comprehension of the world, even so is God far more passionate than we are in having us come to the fullness of life. As imperfect as we are, we naturally work towards our children's happiness. Likewise, God's wish is for us to enjoy his blessings thoroughly and deeply. But we can't enjoy great health living on junk food; nor can we enjoy the fullness of God's blessing if we are fine with living like the world. "You are to be perfect, as your heavenly Father is perfect" (Matthew 5:48).

We have to go beyond submission to God, resisting the devil, drawing near to God, washing our grubby hands and purifying our wayward hearts.

James desires us to be as *emotional* about repentance as we were about getting our own way! Consider his next words:

Be miserable and mourn and weep;
let your laughter be turned into mourning,
and your joy to gloom. (4:9)

I suspect that this call to a "sackcloth and ashes" kind of response—which seemed so natural and occurred so frequently in the Old Testament—is significantly foreign to most of us. In reading along in this passage, I almost miss even *seeing* this verse. There's so little in my personal and cultural experience which resonates with what James says here. Our society does everything it can to avoid the reality of death, and it certainly minimizes the process of grieving— almost to the extent of denying it as a valid experience.

Beyond the foreignness of this behavior, Christians may reason that if one of the fruits of the Spirit is joy (see Galatians 5:22), and if we are commanded so often as Christians to "rejoice" (e.g., 1 Thessalonians 5:16), where does this strong word to "mourn and weep" fit in with the normal Christian life?

As I visualize the occasional clash and friction which arise between parent and son or daughter, I am well aware of the inner antagonism and struggle each side may experience. But what if the parent has this new attitude in mind, the attitude of inner grieving towards God? Grieving because "I am not the man I ought to be," or, "I am not the woman I should be." Grieving, too, because acting the fool brings ruin. It loses the very relational peace and joy we long for; it brings chaos and disorder instead of the taste of paradise we so earnestly desire.

When I listed the character which flows from the "wisdom from above," I posed the question, "Wouldn't every parent like to be described like this: peaceable, gentle, reasonable, full of mercy and good fruits, unwavering, without hypocrisy?"

Does this describe us in our worst moments? Not in our best, but in our *worst* moments? Does our inner life fall short of the character set out as the "fruit of the Spirit"—including such things as patience and kindness and self-control (Galatians 5:22-23)? Then we would do well to mourn.

Jesus once told a story to some people who thought they were doing pretty well, and they viewed others as not quite being up to par (see Luke 18:9–14). In his story, two men went to pray. The religious one—who thought he was doing quite nicely, thank you very much—prayed to himself, thanking God he was not like the usual sinners (swindlers, adulterers, and the like). He wasn't even like that other man standing nearby praying, who was a known sinner! Better than that, this religious man was decidedly very faithful in all of his religious practices, like fasting and giving to the needy.

The other man was a notorious taxman, a sellout who worked for the oppressive government. This man agreed with the low view all society had of him, and "standing some distance away, was even unwilling to lift up his eyes to heaven, but was beating his breast saying, 'God, be merciful to me, the sinner!' " (v. 13).

Have we sold out to the world by craving pleasure of one kind or another? Have we failed to resist the devil who tempts us to "grab what we can," just like those who live solely for worldly desires? Do we on occasion act, and react, more according to our flesh—the sinful nature—than according to the Spirit? Then we, too, are in the position of that sinner. Then we, too, are in need of grieving for our shortcomings and requesting that God would be merciful to us, "For all have sinned and fall short of the glory of God" (Romans 3:23).

Notice that this man in Jesus' story referred to himself as "the sinner." In calling himself this, he was probably not indicating that he was the only, or the worst of, sinners. It's more likely that on his personal horizon, the wretched state of his own life loomed large before him. As far as he was concerned, he really was *the* sinner.

In a similar way, each one of us, when we consider our inner landscape — how impoverished we are in and of ourselves, how easily we react out of our sinful nature, how effortlessly the devil can cause us to stumble, how automatically we can grasp after our own pleasures—we too can be *the* sinner.

This awareness, and acceptance, of our spiritual deadness is just preparation for life. Just as John the Baptist was sent to prepare God's people, so also in our individual lives, before the Messiah comes, comes the call to repentance (see Matthew 3:1-3).

AND AFTER DEATH—*Life*!

The good news is that, despite this grim prognosis, despite the destitution of both our inner and outer life, Jesus said that it was this *sinner* who went home justified. He also added a word of explanation: "For everyone who exalts himself shall be humbled, but he who humbles himself shall be exalted" (Luke 18:14). This echoes the same perspective James includes in repeating the main point of his exhortation: "Humble yourselves in the presence of the Lord, and He will exalt you" (4:10).

This attitude of inner grieving towards God—grieving because "I am not what I ought to be"—can revolutionize the relationship between parent and son or daughter. Instead of the antagonism and struggle exploding, and the fallout worsening once again our relationships, the emotion and energy has already gone into grieving before God over our destitute condition.

As we grow aware of our condition, of how inconsistent or "double-minded" we are in trusting God, of how easily we slip into jealousy or selfish ambition, then we are in a position of moving forward from this inner mess. But the way forward entails not only awareness, but full acceptance of the truth of our state. The necessity of both becoming fully *aware* of oneself, and also of *accepting* what we would rather deny, is quite thematic in spiritual and counseling-related writings. (For me, these crystallized in my own thinking as "steps one and two" from the first two "pillars" in Nathaniel Braden's book, *The Six Pillars of Self-Esteem*, see pp. 66-67.)

Many people are willing to admit, "I'm not perfect." Yet they think to themselves—much like the religious person in Jesus' story—that they are not really as bad as those wretched sinners and criminals. But it is only as we come to a fuller awareness, and humble ourselves to accept the truth of our destitute and disordered hearts—our inner poverty—that we can properly grieve.

This awareness and acceptance can then put us in the position of confessing our condition to God. "If we say that we have no sin, we are deceiving ourselves" (1 John 1:8). Confession will bring about two results: "If we confess our sins, [God] is faithful and righteous to *forgive* us our sins and to *cleanse* us from all unrighteousness" (v. 9, emphasis mine).

Weeping and mourning, sackcloth and ashes—these things are utterly foreign to most of us in our daily lives. But this has been a customary practice for Christians, the practice of fasting. When Jesus instructed his disciples about their regular religious practices—almsgiving, prayer, and fasting (see Matthew 6:1–18)—He never intended them to stop these practices. His point was for them to do these "in secret," to be seen by their Father in heaven, instead of doing them for show, to be seen by others.

In the numerous and culturally varied Christian and church circles I have known, two of these practices have certainly been well-emphasized. It's common to encourage, even to expect, the "giving of alms"—that is, giving money for the poor and needy. And it's usual to exhort and stress our need for engaging in prayer. However, just as the culture at large avoids such difficult topics like grief, mourning and death (as Martin and Ferris point out, pp. ix, 14-18, 102), there has been a notable silence concerning fasting.

This silence about fasting, and its natural companions of weeping and mourning, needs to be broken, for sin and its fallout wreak havoc.

Marriages, families, and entire societies are ruined because of the relentless pursuit after pleasure, ambition, and pride. Grieving for physical pain is natural, even instinctive. Grieving for relational brokenness and emotional pain is also natural, but we tend to avoid dealing with such deep suffering. We may have grown up unaware of, or even denying, such pain; but what family has escaped the ravages of relational sin and spiritual darkness, what child can comprehend the magnitude of our common plight?

In calling his readers to grieving, James opens a way for all of us to turn from "earthly" and "demonic" ways of relating to others. Anyone who deliberately and consistently cultivates this attitude, with respect to their wayward and faithless heart before God, in the long run will not continue to suffer from the same inner mess. Why? "God is opposed to the proud, but gives *grace* to the humble" (James 4:6, emphasis mine). Moreover, God has promised to *cleanse* those who confess to him (see 1 John 1:9).

We have a choice: Either we can do violence to others in the pursuit of our own desires, or we can do violence to ourselves in the pursuit of God's desire. As one Christian writer put it so well, "Man must do violence to his own heart if it is to become faithful" (Padovano, 209).

Within the family, there can be light, and there can be darkness. The light can be wonderful, life-giving, and healing; but the darkness can be terrifying, debilitating, and ruinous. Even though we were born into the darkness of a world pervaded with sin and its aftermath, and even though we reacted—usually without thinking—to the incompleteness and inconsistency of others with our own lack of faith, yet we can still turn to God.

We do not have to pass on to our children the darkness which pervades our own hearts. Even though our children may at times make us expose some of our many deficiencies— our lack of love, and purity, and peace, and patience, and goodness—yet they are not our enemies for inadvertently revealing the state of our hearts. Rather, they can be used by God as a reminder of our need for him, and of the distance which still remains between ourselves and the Source of all goodness and light.

A COMMON FOE

If it's not the kids against whom we war, how then do they fit into this battle scene?

They too are confronted by the very enemies which array themselves against the parents. They too are besieged by the world and its godless perspectives and values, by their own developing "flesh," and by the devil and his spiritual forces. They need—like us—to combat evil and darkness.

Parents, together with their kids, are co-combatants.

Although we are *over* our children in care and authority, we are *together* with them in learning from God, and in needing grace. Just as no one can decide to sit at a piano and suddenly play some complex classical music like that of Beethoven, so the skills and knowledge needed to launch out into life take many, many years to develop. Parents are an essential part of this process; they are necessarily over and beyond the kids.

But still, each child will quickly begin to build his or her own response to God. They will need to learn to trust God in little ways, and for little things. Inescapably, each child will also have his or her own unique development of "the flesh"; their inner attitudes and responses to life's difficulties, opportunities and desires, which will grow up separated from a foundation of unquestioned trust and reliance upon God. This is where some of the spiritual battle will take place. What often seems like a battle between parent and child is sometimes a battle between their egos, or their individualized sinful natures (the "flesh").

If this parent-son/daughter conflict can be seen, not in terms of the people involved, but in terms of either battling, or going along with, "the world, the flesh, or the devil," then much harm can be avoided, and much good may be gained.

God has been drawn into the picture. Indeed, there is the increased awareness of the spiritual nature and aspect of much of our conflicts. The character we would have as parents can be found in the wisdom which God is willing to so generously give. The ugly root of our conflicts has been exposed as growing out of our own jealousies and selfish ambitions.

Our response to this is a continuous one. We must constantly turn from our instinctive grasping after desire, resist the temptations of the devil, humble ourselves before and draw near to God, turn from known sinful activities, set our heart-trust on God alone, and grieve over our impoverished hearts and the ruin of our demonic reactions.

Any parent who has this perspective on conflict, and makes a constant practice of these things, cannot long see their kids as being their enemy—even occasionally. The source of struggle is from within. For both parents and children, our enemies are the spiritual forces of darkness; darkness within, and darkness without.

The Low Road

The journey from war to remembrance can be exceedingly long. The home does not need to be a war-torn battleground of antagonism, ever-deepening between all involved. If we remember who the enemy is, we—husband, wife, children— can band together; we can work together against our common foes. "The weapons of our warfare are not of the flesh, but divinely powerful for the destruction of fortresses" (2 Corinthians 10:4).

Humility is a great strength. It leaves one open and approachable by "children" of all ages. It opens up our relationship with God, and with others. In place of the wreckage wrought by our foolishness, humility takes the poison of the flesh—our sinful nature—and defuses it in open confession before God. Humility also carries with it the promise that God himself will give grace and will exalt us at the proper time. The blessing, and the joy, which we would all hope for in both marriage and family is very near to those who—as the prophet of old put it—"do justice, love kindness, and walk humbly with [their] God" (Micah 6:8).

Biblical Illustrations and Teaching

1. In Psalm 24:3–5, the writer asks the leading question, "Who may stand in [the Lord's] holy place?" (i.e., in the presence of the Lord). James echoes the perceptions of this psalm in urging us to "draw near to God" with clean hands and a pure heart (James 4:8). Do you naturally connect purity with relational closeness? How might this connection affect you in church, in prayer, etc.?

2. Most of the qualities mentioned in the Beatitudes of Matthew 5:3–9 are echoed in James (see 3:17-18; 4:9). Do you regularly associate these qualities with "happiness"? Why, or why not? How could your understanding of these be more aligned with that of Scripture?

3. In the final Beatitude (Matthew 5:10–12), Christ spoke of persecution because of a believer's identification with Christ. What antagonism have you witnessed arising between parent and a son or daughter primarily because one of them is a Christian? In the midst of this, did you continue to witness the character of "the wisdom from above" (see the passages noted in #2 above)?

Little Exercises

1. "The journey from war to remembrance can be exceedingly long." What little exercises could you develop and follow which would help in attempting to make any of the exhortations found in James 4:7–10 an integral part of your Christian walk?

2. List ways in which people experience jealousy, and areas in which they may pursue selfish ambitions (see James 3:14, 16). How might these things give rise to "disorder and every evil thing"? How can these things be given up?

3. With James 4:3 in mind, specify, first, ways in which people may lust (as in having "excessive or immoderate desires") and do not have, so they commit "murder"; and, second, items for which prayers are made for selfish reasons. Do any of these highlight areas in your own life where you may need to become more balanced in your wants, to behave differently, or to change your prayers?

Chapter 10

Save the World – Mend the Fence

The Journey from Messiah to Disciple

*Peter, seeing the disciple whom Jesus loved
said to Jesus, "Lord, …what about this man?"
Jesus said, "… what is that to you?
You follow **Me**"*
John 21:21, 22 (emphasis and rendering mine)

Endless Perfection

"If you don't do it, nobody else will."

"In our church, 20% of the people do 80% of the work—*always!*"

"Last week we came across another village. We preached the gospel—and *thousands* were saved! Then it was off for another five-day trek through the jungle to the next village."

Heroes of the faith. Hardworking. Always on the go. New projects abounding. Dozens of activities to report. Hard-pressed to keep on top. Always, the unexpected—but necessary—people and situations popping up, delaying "the work"; but never for long!

The perfect Christian, the missionary with a halo, the Christian worker extraordinaire, the life given as a whole offering, burnt out for Jesus.

It's an old tug-of-war, the dilemma of depth and breadth; should you be eternally available to the many, or to only a few? You've said "yes" to God, you shocked yourself by saying "yes" to the call for Christian service—down the road, across the world—and now you feel like you need to say "yes" to every person, and request, that comes along!

You've learned the "yes" word, and now— you've forgotten the "no" word.

The pastor asks for volunteers, the needs are endless, the agencies helping the impoverished never stop asking for money — and on and on it goes.

The road to perfection seems endless. There's always something else you should be doing. When will it stop? We have one Lord, and a thousand bosses (really, anybody who walks through the door with yet another thing for us to do); all urgent, all important, all with *your* name written on it.

Or is this all a fantasy, somebody else's dream, somebody else's *life*—or two or three of them? With all the things that need to be done, are you really "the One" who's destined to save the world?

So, here's the Big Question:

What happens to marriage and family while you're out there being the superhero?

Sure, the desperate and needy appreciate the lift—at least that's the way it seems; the marginal and powerless always give face to the powerful and positioned.

But what about the "marginalized and dependent" back home? Those who look to you—yes, *you!*—in a completely unique way, like nobody else on the planet. They look to you for strength, wisdom, setting the mood and tone of the home, and for just being an ordinary person they like being around. Yes, what about them? Do they count as part of your Christian service for God?

How are we to view the relationship of ministry outside of the home to the needs and opportunities inside the home? How did Christ and the apostles—the founder of the Church, and the original "founding fathers"—regard their own ministries? By seeing how these models of our faith regarded their own ministries, we can gain a helpful perspective on our own works of service. We can also see how ministry relates to our commitments and opportunities at home.

In addition to the above, what are the sorts of things which can, and often do, take place *within* the setting of home and family, but which indeed better train us for "outside" service? How can ministry and marriage complement and build upon each other, instead of competing for our time and energy?

There's no place like home to develop as a Christian. But before we consider the present, we'll look to the past. We begin by turning back to the initial heroes of the faith.

THE INITIAL HEROES

If there was anybody who should have felt the urge to save the world, it certainly would have been the original apostles. Handpicked by Christ, present at his incredible miracles, privy to his most intimate teachings, and commissioned to "make disciples of all the nations" (Matthew 28:19), these twelve were set up for burnout before they even started! But did they? Did they feel the need, the driving necessity, to "do it all"?

There was a time when things were getting busy, the church was growing, and as usual, issues arose in the midst of increasing numbers. In this situation, it appeared that some widows of the Greek-speaking Jews were being ignored in favor of the Hebrew-speaking ones in the daily serving of food (see Acts 6:1-7). How did the Twelve respond? Did they say, "Okay, *we'll* take care of this. We'll make sure things are done right around here! Golly, 'If you don't do it yourself, it just won't get done right'!"?

The apostles did nothing of the sort. Instead, they opened their brief comments to the congregation with the remark, "It isn't right for us to neglect the word of God in order to serve tables" (Acts 6:2 rendering mine). They went on to direct the group to select from amongst themselves seven men "of good reputation, full of the Spirit and of wisdom" (v. 3) whom the apostles then put in charge of the "table" ministry. And then, stating their own mission again —for the second time in a mere three verses!—they concluded by saying, "But *we* will devote ourselves to prayer, and to the service of the word" (Acts 6:2–4, emphasis and rendering mine).

Ah, the fine art of delegation. These apostles knew their task. They were clear on what they should say "yes" to, and to what they needed to say "no." They were a focused group.

The apostle Paul had this same kind of focus. Even though he could say, "I have become all things to all people" (1 Corinthians 9:22, NRSV), it wasn't because he was *doing* all things for all people. Paul had this remarkable flexibility towards all things cultural and religious because he knew, and was focused on, his own task. He had become all things to all people, so that he "might by all means save some" (v. 22, NRSV).

The apostles had a task which had been defined by God. As Peter explained in his conversation with the Gentile Cornelius, "We are *witnesses* of the all the things [Jesus] did.... [and] God raised Him up . . . and granted that He should become visible ... to *witnesses* who were chosen beforehand by God, to us, who ate and drank with Him after He arose from the dead. And He ordered us to *preach* to the people ... [and] to *testify* that this is the One appointed by God" (Acts 10:39–42, emphasis mine). This was the central role of the apostles; they were witnesses who were to testify of the earthly life and resurrection of Christ.

The apostles did not try to be the entire Church, with all the gifts, and all the roles and all the offices which eventually came into being. Rather, the apostles had a specific role to play, and they did that one task.

When Paul was dealing with a church divided as to favorite leaders—including himself, Apollos, Cephas and Christ (see 1 Corinthians 1:12)—he explained his own role in very simple terms:

> *What then is Apollos? And what is Paul? Servants through whom you believed....I planted, Apollos watered, but God was causing the growth. ...According to the grace of God which was given to me ... I laid a foundation, and another is building upon it.*
>
> (1 Corinthians 3:5-6, 10)

Paul saw himself as a servant. His task was to lay the foundation of the gospel, and his preference was to do so where the gospel had not yet been heard (as he mentions in Romans 15:20). Although he later lists a good number of gifts, ministries and effects which could be found in a church (see 1 Corinthians 12:4–6, 28–30), he certainly did not claim to have them all. Indeed, only a few applied to him; as he specifically outlines elsewhere, he "was appointed a preacher and an apostle and a teacher" for the gospel (2 Timothy 1:11).

The apostles—those initial "heroes of the faith"—had a specific role to play in God's economy. They did not try to *do* everything, for that would have distracted them from their primary task. They knew what they were to be doing, and that's what they did. Their attitude was like what Christ had pointedly taught them when he ended a lesson with this directive: "So you too, when you do all the things which are commanded you, say, 'We are unworthy slaves; we have done only that which we ought to have done' " (Luke 17:10).

These are the initial heroes, the founding fathers, the ones upon whose witness the whole Church was founded. They didn't do everything; they didn't even try. They had a defined view of their task: "I'm doing *this*, not *that*." Their focus was on that one thing which had been specifically given to them to do. This is how they followed Jesus in the duration of their life service for him.

THOSE WHO PRECEDE, THOSE WHO FOLLOW

The apostles viewed their ministry as something larger than their own efforts; they saw it in terms of both a community and a history of others who were also engaged in the work of God. They learned this from Jesus, and from the stories about Jesus with regard to his own ministry. Both Christ and his apostles saw their service for God in the context of those who had gone before them, and of those who would follow after them.

In the well-known story of Jesus and the unnamed woman at the well (see John 4:1-42), Jesus spoke to the disciples about both his work and their own work with respect to the "harvest" of people who were coming to faith. Because of what the women had told them about Jesus, the men of the city came to find out for themselves whether or not Jesus was the Christ. And as they were approaching, possibly as they were coming into view, Jesus said to his disciples, "lift up your eyes, and look on the fields, they are ripe for harvest" (v. 35 rendering mine).

How did Jesus—the Messiah, the long-awaited one, the "Savior of the world" (as the men of the city later put it, v. 42)—how did he see *his* role in this specific drama? Did he need to start from scratch with these men, as though he was alone in this process of harvesting, of bringing these people to faith? Not at all! Jesus was harvesting, but others had "sown the seed" before he arrived: "Already he who reaps is receiving wages, and is gathering fruit for life eternal; that he who sows and he who reaps may rejoice together. For in this case the saying is true, 'One sows, and another reaps' " (vv. 36-37).

A similar situation had happened at the beginning of Jesus' public ministry, with John the Baptist. John had been sent by God to "make ready a people prepared for the Lord" (Luke 1: 17)—that is, for the coming Christ—by calling them to repentance. In Matthew's Gospel, Jesus' first public appearance is described in terms which echo the previous appearance of John the Baptist. First John, and then Jesus, appeared with the same message, summarized in Matthew with the same words: "Repent, for the kingdom of heaven is at hand" (Matthew 3:2; 4:17). John prepared the people for Jesus, and Jesus picked up right where John had left off.

As with Christ, so with the apostles. Jesus ended his discussion with the disciples about the woman at the well with a comment about the ongoing work of these disciples: "I sent you to reap that for which you have not labored; *others have labored*, and *you have entered into their labor*" (John 4:38, emphasis mine).

In their role of witnesses to Jesus as the Christ, the apostles were building on the work of many who had preceded them. This reality can be seen in the story of the spread of the gospel in Acts. When he was addressing the church in Jerusalem, James noted this widespread work of many: "For Moses from ancient generations has in every city those who preach him, since he is read in the synagogues every Sabbath" (Acts 15:21). The gospel throughout Acts was preached to a prepared audience, for it was, first of all, preached to Jews and God-fearing Gentiles who attended the synagogues on a weekly basis.

Even when he preached to the religiously diverse Gentiles, Paul appealed to the commonality of God's reaching out to all people in every place. God had sent them such natural blessings like rain and sunshine—necessary for survival, good for the crops, etc.—all the while desiring that they search after and find him (see Acts 14:16-17; 17:26-28). The gospel went forth to both Jews and Gentiles whose hearts had been prepared by a rich diversity of means.

The apostles also saw their work being carried on by others. In discussing his own ministry, Paul noted that "I laid a foundation, and *another* is building upon it" (1 Corinthians 3:10, emphasis mine). Paul not only acknowledged that others were building on his work, he actively directed that this should happen. As he wrote to one of his helpers, "For this reason I left you in Crete, that you might *set in order what remains*, and appoint elders in every city as I directed you" (Titus 1:5, emphasis mine). This habit of appointing elders as they established churches appears to have been the regular habit of Barnabas and Paul as they traveled about proclaiming the gospel (Acts 14:23).

In his charge to his "protégé"—Timothy—Paul directed him to continue this tradition of building on the work of some, for yet others to carry on:

Therefore, my son, be strong in the grace that is in Christ Jesus. And the things which you have heard from me ... entrust to faithful men, who will be able to teach others also. (2 Timothy 2:1–2)

From Paul, to Timothy, to some "faithful men," and eventually to "others," the gospel and teaching was to carry on. There is a corporate wholeness here; a community of laborers, spread out in time and spread out in a diversity of places.

Both Jesus and the apostles—even in their pivotal, foundational, and historically unique place in the economy of God—saw their work in the context of those who had preceded them, and of those who were to follow after them. They didn't feel that they had to do it all, or that it was all up to them. Theirs was a defined task. Jesus came to do the will of the Father, which for him entailed giving his life as a "ransom for many" (Matthew 20:28; see also John 4:34). The apostles, as we have seen, were sent out to testify about the life, death and resurrection of Christ.

ONE OF THE BUNCH

If we think that our service for God is all up to us, this can cause incredible anxiety; anxiety which can easily lead to neglecting marriage and family. But learning to see our ministry and service for God in terms of both a community and a history of others who are also engaged in the work of God can ease much anxiety. It can set aside the anxiety which may tempt us to neglect friends and family, marriage and children, all in the name of God. Instead of anxiety, we can exercise faith and hope; faith that God was present and active before we arrived, and hope that God will raise up others who will continue to build after we have left any particular ministry.

Waiting on God is an exercise of faith, and of hope. If we don't wait on God, we will rush about with great anxiety—believing those voices which tell us, "It's *all* up to *you*," as if we were the first Adam, about to affect the entire human race. The hopes and dreams we have for a ministry may be the very valid fuel which keeps us at it; but in the midst of any "labor of love," we must continue to exercise our "work of faith" and "steadfastness of hope" (1 Thessalonians 1:3).

Consider how this was so profoundly put in *Dawn with out Darkness*:

> *It is wrong when we have a timetable for the fulfillment of our most profound expectations. It is wrong when we look for one lifetime to settle the human heart, quiet its every fear, meet its expectations, and end its waiting....*
>
> *We are made to wait because hope and faith are at issue in our waiting....*
>
> *We wait so that we may know that all does not originate with ourselves, not even the meaning of our lives. We wait so that other persons might participate in the process of our lives....*
>
> *A Christian ... chooses to wait. He waits because he knows that life grows in the daylight and in the darkness....A Christian waits because he has seen the lilies, the wheat fields, and the stars....A Christian waits because he knows that even the darkness is a creature of God and that no darkness can withstand dawn.* (Padovano, 86, 90)

In the mist of the "wheat fields" of ministry opportunities, we need to remember how God cares for the "lilies of the field," and the promise of God's care for our immediate needs (see Matthew 6:25-34). We also need to remember how Abraham looked to the stars and believed God's promise regarding his future, that he would indeed make from him a nation—in due time (see Genesis 15:5-6).

Faith and hope are antidotes for the anxiety which tempts us to neglect marriage and family in the name of God, for the "cause" of ministry. With the example of Christ the Savior of the world, and of the apostles who were commissioned to "make disciples of all nations" (a daunting task if ever there was one), husbands and wives the world over can serve without anxiety, and with steadfast patience, knowing that they are not solely responsible for saving the world. Some have preceded them in this task; others will follow after.

Ultimately, no ministry is "up to me." The Spirit gives the gifts for ministry, Christ (the Lord, the head of the Church) directs people into ministries, and God brings about the effects from ministries (see 1 Corinthians 12:4-6). It is God who oversees, directs, empowers and brings to fruition any ministry; our role is to relax, and do what is before us. We are part of a very large group, in both "time and space," throughout history and in a vast diversity of situations. In this context, we can work without anxiety.

TIE YOUR OWN SHOELACES

Because of our hope and trust in God, no Christian needs to neglect marriage or family for the cause of ministry. We don't need to neglect one area of responsibility for another. It is tempting, sometimes, to mix our priorities, to think we are doing a service for God while setting aside those who require our care and attention. "Saving the world" can be a heady task, demanding sacrifices all round; but dare we sacrifice that which God has instituted, marriage and family? Are these really *ours* to give, or to give up? Can we claim to love our neighbor if we neglect those who are near to us? Is God pleased with such sacrifices?

When Paul was directing Timothy about the care of widows, he specifically mentioned how families should take care of their own: "If a widow has children or grandchildren, they should first learn their religious duty to their own family and make some repayment to their parents; for this is pleasing in God's sight" (1 Timothy 5:4, NRSV). And later he adds, "Whoever does not provide for relatives, and especially for family members, has denied the faith and is worse than an unbeliever" (v. 8).

Jesus scorned those who offered to God that which should have been used to care for their parents. "Hypocrites" is the strong term he used to describe those religious leaders who allowed for this practice of giving money to the temple, instead of "honoring" parents through supporting them (see Matthew 15:1-7). Throughout both the Old and the New Testaments, God is most assuredly and strongly on the side of the needy, and of the dependent.

What was stated so boldly by Christ and by Paul with respect to the care of one's aging parents could certainly be applied to the care of one's other family members—including spouse and children. And would we be so inhuman to reduce our obligations to mere monetary provisions? The care and feeding of our closest members may begin with the physical necessities, but true care and nurture—especially of spouse and children—must reach into the depths of their very souls.

And what if we have neglected those to whom we are duty bound? Better to make and ensure reconciliation and peace than to offer religious sacrifice to God. In speaking about broken relationships, Jesus said, "So when you are offering your gift at the altar, if you remember that your brother or sister has something against you, leave your gift there before the altar and go; first be reconciled to your brother or sister, and then come and offer your gift" (Matthew 5:23-24, NRSV).

This is not an either-or situation, as in "either we serve God, or we take care of our own." Jesus condemned the religious leaders for obsessing over religious service, to the neglect of compassion:

> *Woe to you, scribes and Pharisees, hypocrites! For you tithe mint and dill and cummin, and have neglected the weightier provisions of the law: justice and mercy and faithfulness; but these are the things you should have done without neglecting the others.* (Matthew 23:23)

This is a situation which anyone can fall into: Caught up in the details of service, micro-managing our offerings to God—like the "attention to detail in trifling matters like the herbs from the garden" (Beare, 455)—and neglecting what is fair, kind, and of faith. How easy it is to neglect those near to us while focusing so "Christianly" on those outside our family to whom we are endlessly giving help.

Just as we so habitually tie our own shoelaces and take care of ourselves, so we are to just as naturally take care of our own family members. We cannot neglect those near to us, those who look to us as one who fills a unique role in the family. We cannot farm out to others that which only we can give.

Of course, the needs and requirements of a specific spouse, and of specific children, are as varied as the individuals involved. This diversity, though, calls for *more* attention, not less. The opportunities to minister and to care within marriage and family are as unique as each person and each relationship.

Once we are in them, marriage and family are part of life's "given-ness." They bring with them unavoidable responsibilities and unrepeatable opportunities. God evidently places at least as much weight—if not more—on our love expressed to those at home as he does to our "love" and service expressed to those outside of our home.

To sacrifice marriage and family in the name of "Christian" service is wrong; we must pay what we have vowed—as the wise man put it so bluntly in Ecclesiastes 5:4. A neglected marriage, a handful of deprived children, these cannot be the sacrifices with which God is pleased. Rather, love and minister to those at home as they need it—and as you may so naturally desire—without neglecting the love and service to those outside of your home as well. If there is a conflict of time and energy, home has to have priority; for outside needs and opportunities are endless, and in the home is your deepest and most unique arena of service. You will affect no others as deeply, or as foundationally, as you do those at home.

For the most part, the choice will not be an "either-or"; there is usually no need to utterly give up on serving God "out there" in order to care for those at home, according to the needs and opportunities of the moment. What I am arguing against here is the practice, and the teaching—usually indirect and by example—of those who would neglect their home responsibilities as they busy themselves in "the work of the Lord." With such neglect God is, evidently, not pleased. Fortunately for everyone who engages in any unseen acts of service, all such offerings of love, well and truly rendered, usually only strengthen other more visible acts of service. That which is sown in the darkness of obscurity is seen, noted and rewarded by God, even if it is for the "little ones" back home — "little" in physical stature, public role, or personal, emotional or spiritual dependency (see Matthew 6:4, 6, 18; 10:42).

Tie up your own laces, and those of your young children. Don't neglect the needs of those who are growing well, and those who look to you for strength, support, wisdom, and just plain, ordinary fun and "being there." And then, I think, you will be free—yes, *free* — indeed, better equipped, to "go and love and serve the Lord" to those who live outside the walls of your home.

HOME AS REAL PRACTICE

There's no place like home to develop as a Christian. So much of what which is normally hidden from our eyes can come out in the home environment to startle us. There is sometimes a large distance between our fondest hopes, expectations and dreams, and the realities we live in. The ideas we have about ourselves are sometimes vastly different from what happens in the heat of the moment. This can happen in bad ways, of course, like, "I never thought I would react that way!" It can also happen in good ways. Abilities and ways of helping we never dreamed of having or doing suddenly come to light as needs are thrust upon us.

What can the realities of home life teach us about ministry? A considerable amount! The sheer discipline of character required for the unending 24/7 necessity of loving faithfulness is alone more than almost anything one will meet "out there." The in-your-face needs, and the potential of opportunities inherent in both marriage and children, demand of any person more strength, grace, and wisdom than most have naturally available. In this pressure cooker of Christian virtue and service, many things can grow evident about both home and ministry; some quickly, others becoming clearer more slowly, over time. A few of these are considered below.

There & Then, Here & Now

Our control and influence are only relative, both at home and out of the home. Regardless of what position we hold within a family system, no one can "control" another without that other person going along with it; whether they do so deliberately or without much thought. In the long run, our influence is also relative; life goes on, those at home meet people other than ourselves, they experience more of life. And to add to this, there is a built-in limit (which most avoid thinking about) to all that we can do; the eventual "limit" of death, which is built in to all of life.

How does this relate to "saving the world" out there and "mending the fence" back home? As the above reflections on Christ and the apostles have indicated, no one person is responsible, or able, to save the world. Even those most pivotal persons involved in God's economy were linked to those who had gone before them, and to those who would follow after them. Most of us don't get to play such pivotal roles, except in very local, limited situations.

And one of those local, limited situations is marriage; another is family. One conversation, one relationship, may lead one other to Christ. Or it may deepen another's faith, hope, and/or love. That one other person may eventually affect many. Each person in our range of relationships may reach the world. It is at least certain that each person we know can reach into "worlds" of relationships and situations other than what we could ever have access to by ourselves.

We cannot be everywhere, nor—even if we were there—could we do everything. Recognition of this God-imposed limitation on every person is humbling. It can also give rise to gratitude, thanksgiving and prayer. Give thanks for what others are doing, for things which you could never do, in various geographical places, with such a diversity of people and languages and cultures and subcultures. And even for those who are doing what you could do, give thanks; for you are not there, but here. Even electronic images and written words cannot replace the flesh and blood reality and presence of those who are where you are not.

"Bloom where you're planted," my father was fond of saying. The humility implicit in this saying can help a person live in the present, instead of "chasing after the wind" (an expression common in Ecclesiastes). The dream of having other influences, other ministries, other tasks—eventually, being with other people—can be a distraction from serving God where you are. Contributing your unique part to a specific marriage, to particular children, is as much a service to God as is preaching to the thousands.

God regarded even the everyday, common work of the nameless slave in the ancient Roman Empire as a service to himself. Paul said to such slaves, "It is the Lord Christ whom you serve" (Colossians 3:24; see also Ephesians 6:5-8). Nothing is lost; our control and influence is limited, but God sees all that we do, and he receives *all* that is done in serving others as significant service rendered unto himself—including the routine and "unrewarding" tasks that marriage and family entail.

We are not the Messiah, here to save the world; we are only disciples, living in a certain time and place, with certain people. This marriage, this family, is our context for blooming; this, and not another.

Let Your "Yes" Be "Yes"

And what does "yes" mean, but a thousand "no's"? This quickly becomes evident in marriage. Saying "yes" to that one person, even before marriage, even in dating and spending time together, only the two of you, this "yes" of having your own time and space necessitates a "no" to giving the same time and space to others. In saying "yes" to one person in marriage, you are saying "no" to all others—potential or real—who may occupy that *same* place in your heart and life. This exclusivity guarantees depth, intimacy, breadth, stability, rootedness, growth, joy, and much more as the two—as only *these* two—live and learn and grow together.

This depth in one relationship rules out being always available for everyone else. Only God can be eternally available—the rest of us have to sleep sometime. The exclusivity of marriage, and the demands of a developing family, entail time and energy; they require "being there," as well as "doing for." This means that the same time and energy cannot be given to other people. Marriage and family require us to humble ourselves in accepting a limited role in other tasks and relationships.

Depth at home does not diminish impact abroad; in fact, it can often increase it. One can grow in the service of this one person, or those few people. We can grow in overcoming self, overcoming the world, resisting the devil. We can grow in the spirit of "power and love and discipline" (2 Timothy 1:7). The ability to profoundly influence any one person's life "out there" in a moment of time, is often developed in the practice—day in, day out—of being profoundly involved in the life of one person at home.

That "yes" to an exclusive relationship may mean "no" to other relationships of the same kind; but it certainly doesn't do away with the potential of great, or even greater, impact on the lives of others. The master of any discipline who has been subject to rigorous training is uniquely positioned to profoundly, and uniquely, impact learners and students. Depth and exclusivity of training is actually *required* for attaining such influence.

Likewise, those who would desire to minister to others may find considerable training in the "exclusive" arena of marriage and family. After all, the development and conscious exercise of faith, hope and love likely reach greater personal depth in relationships at home than they do almost anywhere else. What one "loses" in such individualized service can be more than offset in the gain of depth and impact.

We are not the Messiah, we are only disciples; limited in time and resources, willing to serve those with whom God has blessed us, at home as well as abroad. The "loss" of serving a few, out of obedience to Christ, may well be offset by the gain of depth of character, and of depth of impact on the lives of others. The simplicity of "yes and "no," aside from purifying our hearts from excessive egotism, can deepen our life in the Spirit, and result in a flow of fresher water to those who thirst for eternal life (see Matthew 5:37; John 7:38).

GIVE ME SOME SPACE!

The outcome is uncertain. After all those years of input, care and nurture, admonitions and exhortations and directions given times without number, you cannot control what will come of all your hard work. Children can pass their courses at school, but will they ever look at that subject again? Kids can show up at church and youth group and retreats, but will they follow Jesus when life narrows down to a single file, when the pathway becomes one-on-one?

The same question can be asked of one's spouse. Having begun well—as well as it seemed back when you began together—will both of you individually continue to follow the way of God?

These questions may bring a sense of sadness, for many have grown up in the church, within the sound of solid teaching, and yet at some point—during their youth, or during their adult years as life has unfolded—they have wandered off, or at least pulled back from that heart response to God which eventually changes everything.

Jesus taught that there would be a variety of responses to the gospel. In the parable of the "Sower and the Seed," he outlined four different "soils" onto which the "seed" fell, four different responses to the word of God, the message of the Kingdom. Some hear without understanding, and the devil takes away even what they have heard. Some hear with joy, but fall away when difficult times come. Some hear, but concerns over worries and riches and things choke out the word. The only ones who bear fruit in their lives are those who hear, understand, accept and act on what they have heard (see Matthew 13:18-23; Mark 4:14-20; Luke 8:11-21).

The effect, the outcome, of all your service and labor of love is not up to you; the "soils" play a part in it. It's between them, and God. There is an arena into which no one can enter, except the individual, and God. We may hope, and pray, but the response of an individual to and before God is up to that individual. And who knows? Seed sown unconsciously in a moment of time may come to fruition decades later.

Despite hearing Jesus' teaching, the Pharisees didn't understand his message about the Kingdom. Jesus didn't agonize over this negative outcome, for, as he told his disciples about the Pharisees, "Every plant which my heavenly Father did not plant shall be rooted up. Let them alone" (Matthew 15:13-14). Although Jesus responded to individual Pharisees openly (like Nicodemus, see John 3:1–21), as a group these religious leaders completely missed the new thing God was doing in the person and work of Christ.

A number of times, Paul the apostle voiced the hope that he had not worked "in vain." Regarding the Christians he had left behind in Thessalonica, he sent Timothy "for fear that the tempter might have tempted you, and our labor should be in vain" (1 Thessalonians 3:5). Happily, Timothy could bring back "good news of [their] faith and love" (v. 6). Another time Paul was concerned that the Christian leaders in Jerusalem would not recognize his teaching that Greeks did not have to becomes Jews to be saved, and that he "might be running, or had run, in vain" (Galatians 2:2). Fortunately these leaders were one with him in this issue, and the gospel was not compromised in any way.

Christian leaders, new disciples, the religious leadership — any of these may miss the way of God. Part of faith is inactivity, the discipline of *not* doing, of just letting people respond as they will. Part of the profound respect which is found in Scripture for the individual is that he or she is "allowed" to wander off, to lose the way, to miss what God has done or is doing.

This inactivity, this respecting a person's freedom to respond, is not unconcern. Jesus taught and debated and rebuked those who couldn't or wouldn't "get" that God was doing something new in Christ. Paul reasoned, argued, persuaded and rebuked those Jews throughout Acts who still weren't persuaded that Jesus was the Christ.

Part of our being a disciple is not only to follow Jesus, but we also act to encourage our spouse—and our children—in their individual responses in following as well. Part of not having a "messiah complex" is leaving them room to respond to God in their own way, in their own time. The outcome of our efforts is uncertain, and our control and influence are limited. But we can still be fully involved in the process of loving and serving at home—learning to let our "yes" be "yes" indeed—all the while knowing that each must respond to the Spirit individually, not through any sense of being compelled by anyone, except by God himself.

FROM LOVE TO MARRIAGE

Throughout this book, we have been on a journey, a trip which had a definite point of departure—a foundation to which all other aspects of marriage are related. The movement from that initial tug of love, to a full and complete marriage, is itself a long, long journey. It is a journey into the deepest part of the human psyche, into the depths of our most earnest hopes and dreams, of our ambitions, our expectations, our realizations, our very lives. Where do we start? Upon what do we build? What is the center which makes sense of the whole thing, and all its different parts? We began at the beginning, the foundation, which is also the goal to which we strive.

In the Christian message, there is the firm belief that we cannot be happy apart from having God at the very center of our lives. Our greatest joy is to be found in the relentless pursuit and realization of the first and greatest command: To love God above all other loves.

In our fallen condition, this belief often appears to be completely counterintuitive; it simply doesn't make sense. But apart from God being at the center of both male and female, husband and wife, marriage will be a marriage to—and into—more darkness than light.

In order to complete the journey from love to marriage, we must walk through the valley of death. We must become dead to the world, dead to self, and dead to the powers of spiritual darkness. And the more we are dead to these things which deceive and destroy us, the more we will be alive unto God. And the more we are alive unto God, the more we will enjoy those wonderful blessings, those beatitudes, which are so frequently set before us in Scripture to entice us onward into life.

There's so much involved in this foundational realignment of creature to Creator and the created order. The other things covered in this book, following the first and foundational chapter, are just a few of the many aspects involved in growing into the fullness of a Christian marriage in a Christian way, of journeying from self to the only true center of life—God.

With respect to the life of the soul, Christians should be light-years ahead of most, simply because we are required right at the outset to confess and forsake what we instinctively tend to deny. We are required to move from silence to confession. "If we say that we have no sin, we are deceiving ourselves....If we confess our sins, He is faithful ... to forgive us our sins" (1 John 1:8–9). Our natural resistance to this process, our reluctance to be thorough-going, is revealed in how quickly and easily we cover up within marriage; accusation or silence comes so much more naturally than confession. To maintain growth and communication, we have to make that constant decision to keep open about our inner state as well as our outer activities. Of course, this is done first and foremost before God, but our marriage can deepen and we can experience more healing as we also confess before—and to—one another (see James 5:16).

The humility which arises from realizing our created status before God—and in acknowledging our need for confession—is further deepened by the many implications this involves. Our created minds are limited, as are our darkened hearts. We cannot rely solely on our cleverness to figure out how the created world works, or even how the world of relationships works—like determining who fits best with whom for marriage, or what makes people tick within a marriage. "People ... are not problems to be solved, they are mysteries to be loved" (Pattison, 139). Nor can we simply rely on our gut feelings, moments of ecstatic feelings or our intuitions to make relationships work. God has made us dependant, and in this humility we can be open to learning— from those who God has placed nearby within the community, from the word read, preached or taught, and from the Spirit.

We also need to cooperate with the give-and-take of marriage; neither exalting one person, nor negating the other. Any time the "self" fights to have its own way, it sets itself in opposition to the "community" of marriage. There is no happiness in being disconnected. We were made to be in community, both within and apart from marriage. God at the centre—the very foundation of all things—is the foundation of "two becoming one." In giving of oneself, each becomes more himself and herself, rooted in the everlasting, but serving the other in the here and now.

For any person, any relationship, we need both distance and intimacy to breathe, grow, connect and enjoy. Time spent alone is necessary for any person to become an individual. Time spent alone as a couple is also necessary for the two to become one—long, long after the honeymoon has become a distant memory! In the ebb and flow of living, the world can crush us in its inhuman drive toward noise and clatter and ceaseless activity, wherein all becomes conformity and there is nothing wonderfully unique in either individuals or in relationships. Marriage needs "time out" to survive, thrive and grow into its full glory.

For marriage to blossom and grow, we must constantly check to ensure that we are acting with an ever-deepening respect and with self-sacrificial love. Christ showed us what God is like in his example of being a gentle king, attuned to the needy, wary of the crowd, and committed to his own. This is what we are to be like as well. Is it such a great stretch for husbands to love their wives for the good of the wife, and for wives to respect their husbands whom God has created and redeemed? Of course it is!

Such challenges are why we need to be constantly reminded that our struggles are spiritual ones. It's not our spouse, or the kids, who mess up our lives. It's very helpful to remember, and to be reminded, that we're not in a battle against people—even those at home! We are at war against the ungodly systems of the world "out there," the sinful nature within, and the powers of spiritual darkness which are everywhere.

We do have a role to play in the world, but our roles in marriage and at home are crucial. We are not the Messiah, the Savior of the world. We are not gods. We are called simply to be disciples of Christ; those who follow him, one of the bunch, someone with something to contribute—and a whole lot to receive—within the Church, the Body of Christ. We don't have to give up our marriages to "save the world"; saving the whole world can never be the task of one individual. Our calling is to follow the Savior, and to do well those few, specific tasks he puts before us. But God evidently never intends for our service for him to set aside our family duties—including its joys and opportunities.

Against what the world believes and propagates, the Christian message is clear that God is the way to happiness. I have used the picture of a journey throughout these chapters because it takes most of us a lifetime to advance significantly in the practice of Christian faith, hope and love. There is a great humility implicit in becoming aware of, accepting and responding to the reality of God's truths. This humility is the arena in which true marriage can take place, and within which the happiness and blessing of God can be known and experienced. This journey is long, but for all who embark upon it, the light happily begins to shine early on within our closest relationships, and the reward grows deeper and even more certain as we continue to make progress along the way.

> *The path of the righteous*
> *Is like the light of dawn,*
> *That shines brighter and brighter*
> *Until the full day.*
>
> Proverbs 4:18

Biblical Illustrations and Teaching

1. The limited and defined roles of Christ and the apostles, and how they were connected to the work of others, were set out in the sections on "The Initial Heroes" and "Those Who Precede, Those Who Follow". How might the knowledge of your own limited role, and its connection to the work of others, affect your time and commitment to "Christian work," and to your marriage?

2. In Matthew 23:23, Jesus condemned the religious leaders for being obsessed over the smallest details of religious service, while neglecting compassion. In what ways have you neglected the "weightier" matters of love and

compassion in the pursuit of "religious correctness"? How can you achieve a more balanced life in this regard?

3. In Matthew 6:4, 6, 18 and 10:42, there is mention of how God notes our small and hidden acts of service. What specific home duties could be included in here? Would this include relational times, as well? Why or why not?

Little Exercises

1. List what activities or people compete for your time and energy, and in doing so, work against your marriage. Discuss your part and responsibilities concerning these things. How can you move toward strengthening your role and place within the marriage covenant?

2. How compelled are you in your "Christian service" to ignore spouse and family? Review the passages and discussion in this chapter about how God regards such activities. Are there some priorities which need to be changed? How would this take place?

3. In the final section—"From Love, to Marriage"—which reviews much of the book, trace how humility is an intricate part of what has been set forth in these chapters. Reflect on how humility, of a lack thereof, has affected your own marriage, and the marriages of those you know. How does this affect your desire to grow as a Christian?

Works Cited

Abarbanel, Andrew. *Loving Madly, Loving Sanely.* New York: Kensington Books, 1997.

Beare, F. W. *The Gospel According to Matthew.* San Francisco: Harper & Row Publishers, 1981.

Best, Ernest. *Essays on Ephesians.* International Critical Commentary Series. Edinburgh: T. & T. Clark Publishers, Ltd., 1998.

Braden, Nathaniel. *The Six Pillars of Self-Esteem.* New York: Bantam, 1994.

Crabb Jr., Lawrence J. *Basic Principles of Biblical Counseling.* Grand Rapids: Zondervan Publishing House, 1975.

Crabb Jr., Lawrence J. *Understanding People: Deep Longings for Relationship.* Grand Rapids: Zondervan Publishing House, 1987.

Foster, Richard J., and James Bryan Smith, eds. "E. Stanley Jones." In *Devotional Classics: Selected Readings for Individuals and Groups.* New York: HarperCollins Publishers, 1993.

Godwin, Malcolm. *Who Are You?: 101 Ways of Seeing Yourself.* New York: Penguin Books, 2000.

Gribbin, John. *Almost Everyone's Guide to Science.* London: Weidenfeld & Nicolson, 1998.

Hurding, Roger F. *Roots & Shoots: A Guide to Counseling and Psychotherapy.* London: Hodder & Stoughton, 1986.

Hutchings, Donald. *Late Seventeenth Century Scientists.* Toronto: Pergamon of Canada, Ltd., 1969.

Marshall, I Howard. *Commentary on Luke.* New International Greek Testament Commentary. Grand

Rapids: William B. Eerdmans Publishing Company, 1978.

Martin, John D., and Frank D. Ferris. *I Can't Stop Crying*. Toronto: Key Porter Books, 1992.

Maté, Gabor. *Scattered Minds*. Canada: Alfred A. Knoff, 1999.

McKane, William. *Proverbs, A New Approach*. Philadelphia: The Westminster Press, 1970.

McKenzie, Steven L., and Stephen R. Haynes, eds. *To Each Its Own Meaning*. Kentucky: Westminster/John Knox Press, 1993.

Neander, Joachim. "Praise to the Lord, the Almighty," *The Hymnal for Worship & Celebration*. Waco: Word Music, 1986.

Padovano, Anthony T. *Dawn Without Darkness*. New York: Image Books, 1982.

Pattison, Stephen. *A Critique of Pastoral Care*. London: SCM Press Ltd., 1988.

Ratey, John J., and Catherine Johnson. *Shadow Syndromes*. New York: Pantheon Books, 1997.

Siler, Todd. *Breaking the Mind Barrier*. New York: Simon & Schuster, 1990.

Note: regarding my own rendering of various verses, and any emphasis within such, the original language versions used for this process are as follows:

Alt, A, et al., eds. *Biblia Hebraica Stuttgartensia*. Stuttgart: Deutsche Bibelgesellschaft, 1984.

Aland, Kurt, et al., eds. *The Greek New Testament*. 3rd ed. New York: American Bible Society, 1975.